REVELATION

IMAGES OF CHRIST

REVELATION

IMAGES OF CHRIST

BRIAN WILLIAMS

Revelation: Images of Jesus
© 2025 by Brian Williams

Scriptures taken from the Holy Bible, New International Version®, NIV®. Copyright © 1973, 1978, 1984, 2011 by Biblica, Inc.™ Used by permission of Zondervan. All rights reserved worldwide. www.zondervan.com The "NIV" and "New International Version" are trademarks registered in the United States Patent and Trademark Office by Biblica, Inc.™

Cover Art by Megan Crespo

Published in the United States

For those who dare to imagine

Table of Contents

Introduction	1
The Cosmic Christ	13
The Slain Lamb	30
The Judging Lamb	48
The Saving Lamb	66
The Infant Child	81
The Conquering Christ	98
The Reigning Lord	117
Conclusion	134
Bibliography	139

Introduction

*Imagination is more important than knowledge.
Knowledge is limited. Imagination encircles the world.*
Albert Einstein

The Book of Revelation needs no introduction. Its existence as part of Christian Scripture is widely known. The many horrific and vivid images that fills its pages find their way into all kinds of popular art forms ranging from song, literature, film, painting, graffiti, to body art. It would be nearly impossible to escape the very long reach of Revelation in our daily and ordinary lives. Revelation casts a shadow which stretches the entire length of eternity itself.

From the time of its writing in the late first century, readers of this ancient document have sought to make sense of the various visions and images that emerge from its pages. The sheer range of images stretch from the heights of heaven to the depths of hell, with many of them unfolding on the earth itself. Although images of Revelation find expression in endless ways in nearly every culture, the meaning of these visions and images is often elusive.

There is no shortage of sermons, teachings, and books on Revelation. The volume of resources is more than plentiful. The vast range of interpretations of Revelation stretches from widely populist types of approaches to very academic types of approaches. When populist interpretations of Revelation are viewed side by side with academic interpretations, it might seem as if the populists and the scholars are reading from two different texts altogether.

Given the vastness of resources and the latitude of interpretation, it could easily be argued that there is no legitimate need for another word – much less a book – that is devoted to Revelation. My interest in coming to the text of Revelation is not so much about interpretation as it is about imagination. I am contending that the primary reason there is so much enigma, confusion, and diversity in interpreting Revelation is because there is a lack of understanding how Scripture speaks to the imagination. This is quite different from the wildly imaginative types of interpretations that have been fueled by the images found in Revelation.

The focus of this book is not in offering extensive and elaborate commentary, but in encouraging a certain kind of posture and perspective as we approach Revelation. Typically, readers come to Revelation with either a literalistic lens of interpretation or a literary lens of interpretation. The literalist approach predictably ends up with such things as forced schemes and timelines along with creative connections of Revelation to current events and the evening news. The literary approach is much more in line with the apocalyptic nature of Revelation, but if not appropriately wielded can lead to an imaginary reading which has little to no connection with our historical context.

Taking our cues from the text itself rather than from the imposed paradigms that we place on the text, I will seek to dive into Revelation and invite our imagination to do the heavy lifting. This is not because I am tossing aside any hope of getting to the meaning of Revelation. Rather, I am inviting us to embrace the reality that as unique members of God's creation who are made in the image of God we have been given the gift of imagination. For many readers of Scripture this gift has been undernourished and underutilized. Our approaches to Scripture typically rest in the part of us that thinks rationally and logically – which are also gifts from God. However, a total dependence on them can lead to atrophy of the imagination.

If ever there were a book in the Bible that beckons us to experience God through imagination, it is Revelation. The words on the page make up much more than chapter and verse. In fact, it would be better to read Revelation without the demarcations of chapter and verse. The narrative that is told in Revelation inherently alerts us to the transitions between scenes or changes in scenes altogether. If we are open to letting the Spirit guide our imagination, the words of the text can rise above our analysis of them and transport us to a place where we can – very much like John – see, hear, and experience the unfolding drama not as a distant bystander but as an engaged participant.

The Usual Suspects

Getting from there to here requires that something be done with all the usual suspects. For a number of years, I have had the opportunity to teach the book of Revelation in a variety of settings. Most of the settings were with individuals who had church affiliations and who had some exposure to Revelation. At the beginning of each class, I would perform the same exact exercise. With a large blackboard or whiteboard at my disposal, I asked a very simple question – "What would you like to know about the book of Revelation?"

Inevitably, the responses have been the same throughout the years. Without exception, here are the questions that end up on the board: What does the number 666 mean? Who is the Anti-Christ? What are the signs of the times? When do the events of Revelation take place? What will happen at the Battle of Armageddon? Are we living in the end times? When will the Rapture take place? Who will be in the Tribulation? When is the Second Coming? When does the thousand-year reign of Jesus take place? What happens at the Great White Throne Judgment? What are heaven and hell like?

Although any or all of these questions might be interesting and even entertaining, none of them reflect the purpose and theme of Revelation – not a single one. Revelation was not written because these were the burning questions that were raging like a forest fire through the hearts and minds of John's audience. These were not even the issues God was seeking to reveal to John through visions. In light of the revelation that these popular questions do not reflect the primary purpose of

Revelation, we will not spin our wheels in seeking to address them. The bold setting aside of these popular issues will in fact help make it possible for us to more fully pursue the scent of what Revelation has always been about – the triumph of Jesus Christ over everything!

The dismissal of the most popular questions associated with Revelation forces us to reorient our entire approach to this book. Nearly all of the popular questions are rooted in the same overarching concern – the deep human desire to know what will happen when. In order to satisfy our quest and quench our thirst, we have found ourselves beholden to whatever framework that we can use to place on the text. Once we have settled on the framework, it is easy to let the framework guide our reading rather than allowing the text itself to inform our reading.

Being guided by a framework for interpreting Revelation is what I will refer to as "text management." This is a simple way of saying that because we are not quite sure what to do with Revelation, we set out to manage the text to fit our framework. This is like trying to force our foot into a shoe that does not fit. If we force our foot long enough, we can cram it into the shoe. Popular approaches like dispensation schemes and millennial options all end up doing exactly the same thing – forcing the text into a framework which does not arise from the text itself. As we begin to walk in shoes that don't fit the text, we can usually manage to get from place to place – but at great cost to the intent of the text itself.

The primary reason behind this "text management" approach to Revelation is that we are driven by a deep need to understand the text. In and of itself, seeking to understand the text is not a bad thing. This is exactly what biblical interpretation endeavors to do. The problem is that there are times in which the more we manage a biblical text, the less the text manages us. If Revelation were designed to be a secret code of some kind with a hidden message to Christians, then managing the text to decipher the code would be quite beneficial. We could simply massage the text until we are able to ascertain the hidden message.

Needless to say, the very idea of having to decode Revelation goes against the very notion of revelation itself. The very intent of the act of revelation is that something is *unveiled* – not that something is *veiled*.

Something is *revealed* – not *concealed*. What many readers of Revelation fail to realize is that the *what* which is revealed in Revelation is actually a *who*.

Grand Opening

The purpose of Revelation is not hidden deep within its pages or at the final and dramatic ending. Rather, the purpose is boldly and clearly stated right at the starting line – it is the "revelation *of* Jesus Christ." It is not the revelation of the identity of the Antichrist, the end times, or of a particular millennial model. What is being revealed in Revelation is nothing other than Jesus Christ himself. The preposition "of" in the opening statement could be translated as either the revelation that is *about* Jesus or the revelation that is *from* Jesus. In this case, there is no reason why both are not true. It is a beautiful way for John to express that Jesus is both the revealed and the revealer.

The challenge that most readers of Revelation face is that once they get into the fray of it all, the opening line is long forgotten. As readers make their way through the haze and maze of images, visions, horsemen, seals, trumpets, bowls, numbers, colors, dragons and beasts, and even prostitutes, it can feel like we are just getting off a merry go round and trying to walk a straight line. In those nauseating moments of trying to regain our orientation, we are not sure why we ever got on to begin with. While we are staggering our way through Revelation, we can easily forget that the opening line raises the curtain and shows us in plain sight who is the subject and the object of the entire book from beginning to end.

Once we are reconciled to the notion that Revelation is the revelation "of" Jesus, we can see the entire book in a new and fresh way – which is nothing other than the original way in which Revelation was read. The rather large gap that often separates original readers from contemporary readers is basically one that is rooted in literary genre. The book of Revelation itself includes three various genres – letter, prophecy, and apocalypse.

We are most familiar with the genre of letter or epistle. Consequently, we get the basic idea that John was instructed to write specific letters to seven particular churches in Asia Minor. We can easily locate on a map each of the cities in which these very different churches existed. Although the original churches in these cities are long gone, the cities themselves can still be visited and in many cases ancient ruins of first century life can still be seen.

The genres of prophecy and apocalypse pose more of a challenge for modern readers. There has been a longstanding assumption with many readers – especially those who are more inclined toward populist approaches – that prophecy is primarily a genre that is used for predictive purposes. When this particular view of prophecy shapes our reading of the text, it is easy to see how readers are prone to read Revelation in terms of predictive future. Every image and vision is projected into the future, and every major current event is a fulfillment of a past prediction.

Biblical prophecy – wherever it is found in the Bible – does not have as its primary purpose the prediction of the future. In fact, there is relatively little prediction in prophecy at all. The purpose of prophecy is not so much to predict the future as it is to proclaim what God is saying and doing *now*. The prophets of the Old Testament were far more interested in proclaiming what God was doing rather than in predicting what God was going to do. Prophets spoke powerfully and boldly to the immediate events of the day rather than to the distant events of the future. This is, in fact, why many of the prophets were rejected and killed. It was not because of their predictions of future events, but because of their willingness to speak challenging words of God within their own historical contexts.

When Revelation is read through the lens of a more biblically and historically oriented sort of prophecy, its message can more easily be embraced in terms of things that have already happened and are in fact continuing to happen. For many readers, this notion has fairly revolutionary implications. We do not need to be feverishly looking to the future to see when particular events are to take place. Instead, we can look to every day and every moment of each day as the time and place where God is constantly and faithfully fulfilling his redemptive purpose in Jesus.

The most challenging genre for modern readers is the apocalyptic genre. Although apocalyptic language and images flood our cultural discourse and media, the ability to interpret apocalyptic images and visions in the context of Revelation comes with a boatload of challenge and confusion. One of those challenges is the sheer distance between the first century and the twenty first century. Apocalyptic literature itself was a genre which flourished primarily between 200 B.C. and 200 A.D.

At heart, apocalyptic literature uses exaggerated images to tell stories in dramatic and imaginative ways. The use of apocalyptic language is often problematic to those who take a literalistic approach to Revelation. The whole point of apocalyptic language is to be non-literal. The disconnect for many readers at this point is directly related to the notion of anything in Scripture as being deemed non-literal. For many readers this equates to approaching Scripture as if it were fictitious and untrue.

The use of apocalyptic images does not mean that we have entered into the world of fiction and fairytale. It simply means that in the case of Revelation, apocalyptic language is being used as a medium for writing about real historical persons and events. Apocalypticism simply pulls from a deep well of images that are skillfully and artistically employed to tell the true, historical, and real story of Jesus.

An unavoidably honest question is why would it be necessary to use apocalyptic language to tell a true and real story? Why even cast the story of Jesus in such a way as to bring about confusion, speculation, and division? Would it not be far more simple, clean, and clear just to say it right out loud? Does not all the embellishment and exaggeration get in the way of simply telling the story in its purest form? Why does a narrative that is centered on the triumph of Jesus against evil and the renewal of all things need to be presented in such dramatic and daunting images?

The use of apocalyptic language allows us to see the narrative of Jesus' victory in terms of greater context and deeper texture. It is certainly true that the story of Jesus' triumph could have been told in a far simpler way without us wading through all of the graphic drama. However, it is the very nature and purpose of apocalyptic language to create images which can be housed in our imagination. By aiming its message at our imagination, the narrative of Revelation invites us into a full-orbed drama which embraces the totality of our senses and captures our entire being.

Revelation presents the story of Jesus not as a matter-of-fact kind of objective statement, but as a living and breathing dramatic reality. We can't simply check a theological or doctrinal box that declares that Jesus is the victor – we must engage in the very story which is told in Revelation. Just as our daily lives are filled with so much context and texture of life all around us, so is the story of Jesus filled with even more context and texture of his ongoing victory and ultimate triumph. There is simply no way of telling this story without the use of language that evokes the deepest part of our imagination and speaks to us at places in our lives where normal discourse rarely travels.

The Big Stage

Every narrative unfolds in a certain place, at a certain time, with certain characters, and with a certain plot. The stage on which the narrative is told may be as small as a figment of our imagination or as far flung as the galaxies of the universe. Although the apocalyptic visions in Revelation take place beyond the historical stage, the reality to which the visions point takes place right in the middle of our historical contexts and unfold right in front of us for those who have eyes to see and ears to hear.

The images and visions of Revelation are otherworldly. These images include that of a heavenly being standing among seven golden lampstands; someone sitting on a throne in heaven; twenty four elders dressed in white with crowns of gold on their heads; four living creatures covered with eyes who take various forms of a lion, ox , man, and eagle; a mighty angel; a slain Lamb with seven horns and seven eyes; seven seals of judgment peeled off of a scroll that the Lamb takes from God; seven angels blowing seven trumpets of judgment; a mighty angel holding a little scroll; a pregnant woman clothed with the sun and with the moon under her feet and a crown of twelve stars on her head; an enormous red dragon with seven heads, ten horns and seven crowns; a sea beast with ten horns, seven heads – one of which had been fatally wounded and healed – and ten crowns; an earth beast that has two horns like a lamb but speaks like a dragon; 144,000 people with the name of the Lamb and of the Father written on their foreheads; one like the son of man sitting on a white cloud with a crown of gold on his head and sharp sickle in his hand; seven golden bowls of wrath; a prostitute dressed in purple and scarlet, glittering with gold, precious stones, and pearls; a scarlet beast covered with blasphemous names and having seven heads and ten horns; a rider on a white horse whose robe is dipped in blood and whose name is the Word of God and who has a sharp sword coming out of his mouth and on whose robe and thigh are the words King of Kings and Lord of Lords; a lake of fire; a new heaven and a new earth; the Holy City of Jerusalem prepared as a bride for her husband; the river of the water of life flowing through the middle of the city; and, the tree of life on each side of the river bearing twelve crops of fruit each year.

By any measure, this is quite a bit to take in. Notice that these are just the descriptions. The action and narrative is what takes place in between these descriptions. It is understandable for readers to either reach for the easy button or to bail out at this point. It is no wonder that there is such a plethora of resources that seek to practice text management by stuffing the images into frameworks and timelines that simply don't reflect anything that is actually in the text of Revelation itself. The need to put slippery texts into neat theological boxes is overwhelming. Once we have packaged the text, we can put labels and handles on it so that we can explain the text to others and carry it with us wherever we go.

Revelation, however, refuses to be packaged so that we can fit it nicely into our own theological world. For some this may be a curse, but in reality this is a great blessing for all who would dare come to Revelation with an open imagination, a humble spirit, and a heart to hear what the Spirit is saying to the church.

Perhaps the greatest challenge faced by many readers is that of trying to make any connection between the apocalyptic images and dramatic activity which fill the pages of Revelation with anything that has to do with our discipleship and growth as followers of Jesus. Before we begin our journey through the book of Revelation, let's see if we can make some headway in connecting the dots between an ancient apocalyptic text and the current historical and cultural world in which we live.

Let's just make a bold assertion – Revelation has a lot to do with our current context. It is on this very slippery patch of ice where many readers lose their footing. Although Revelation uses fantastical and otherworldly images as characters in the story, and although the story line may seem distant and fictional, all of this is designed for one purpose – to reveal the past, present, and future redemptive activity of Jesus in our world.

The images of Revelation themselves are not real, but the realities to which they point are quite real! Revelation is a masterpiece which uses literary techniques to reveal literal realities. There is no such thing as a literal red dragon with seven heads and ten horns and seven crowns on its heads. However, there is the very real presence of evil in our world. In the first century world, the center of evil could well be identified with Rome itself and the imperial cult associated with Rome. The dragon may not be real, but the Roman Empire was as real as it got. The activities ascribed to the dragon are fictitious, but the activity of Rome was stretched far and wide across the historical landscape.

Even though the Roman Empire took its last gasp in 476 AD when Emperor Romulus Augustulus was deposed by a German barbarian, the enormous red dragon continues to breathe mightily among nations and rulers. Political, economic, and militaristic evil that finds expression in every generation and throughout the entire world has not lost one step or been abated in any way since the days of the Roman Empire. The dragon continues to breathe death and destruction, and we are subject to its ruinous agenda every single day.

The events of Revelation are unfolding right here and now. Our current historical stage is where the reality of the activity of Revelation is taking place. We are right in the middle of something that is so much greater and so much bigger than we can even imagine – yet it is our very imagination that opens this world up to us. Revelation doesn't transport us to a world that we did not know existed – it reveals a world that fully exists all around us that we might not even know about. It is something like putting on night lens goggles to see what world lurks in the dark. Revelation speaks to a reality that is real even though we are not able to see it apart from the apocalyptic images and visions which allow us to see what we could have never seen otherwise. Perhaps the world which Revelation reveals to us is more real than the world that is before our very eyes.

The Images of Jesus

Jesus is clearly the focus of Revelation. It would be impossible to read through Revelation and not notice the high frequency with which the number seven is used – the seven spirits, the seven stars, the seven angels of the churches, the seven churches, the seven lampstands, the seven torches, the seven thunders, the seven horns and eyes of the Lamb, the seven seals, the seven trumpets, the seven bowls, the seven headed dragon, and the seven headed beast. Each of these sevens are clearly enumerated throughout Revelation.

This book will focus on seven apocalyptic images of Jesus. Although these images are not enumerated, they will be presented in the order in which they appear in the narrative. It is sufficient to say at the outset that although these images are very different, they all point to the one and same Jesus Christ. Just the fact that these images are so bold, dramatic, and unique already alerts us to the reality that no single image of Jesus can fully contain him. The various images are a declaration that the majesty and mystery of Jesus are well beyond our mental and rational capacity. Nevertheless, we can see the beauty, feel the power, hear the voices, smell the aromas, taste the victory of all that Revelation presents to us.

Only a bold imagination shaped by the Spirit of the living God can lead us from image to image. Like looking at a great piece of art, we are invited to behold the images of Revelation until they capture our imagination. I will refer to our approach in reading Revelation as that of *image reading*. This is exactly what apocalyptic literature was originally designed to do.

As I have done in previous works on Acts and Parables, I will refrain from the use of citing chapter and verse. Scripture was not originally written with such demarcations. Although they are certainly helpful in locating a particular story or passage, they can also obstruct our vision of the very image to which they point. As such, we will follow the tradition of the saints of God who were the original readers and hearers of the story.

Every chapter follows the same pattern. The opening section of each chapter, **Behind the Scenes**, is nothing other than a condensed presentation of the text of Revelation itself. The following section, **Historical Stage**, seeks to explore the meaning of the images in the context of historical situation. The **Contemporary Reflection** section identifies basic theological themes and seeks to connect them to our contemporary settings. Each chapter concludes with a **Wrap Up**.

Enjoy the show!

First Image:
The Exalted Christ

Truth is a matter of the imagination.
Ursula K. Le Guin

The opening scene in Revelation is one in which a very cosmic depiction of Jesus is cast against a very earthly depiction of the early followers of Jesus in various communities of faith. Whereas the cosmic Christ is depicted in a heavenly kind of vision, the seven churches of Revelation are scattered across the terrain of Asia Minor. The very cosmic depiction of Christ draws upon a variety of apocalyptic images originally conveyed through the hands of the prophets. The various churches represent communities of faith which are unique and distinct in their specific geographical and historical location.

The one story of the cosmic Christ is set in the context of the various stories of each of the churches. No one of the seven churches is exactly like any of the others. Each church has its own story to tell and each of the churches relate to Christ in their own particular way. Although these are not the only churches that were in existence at the time, they are churches that are geographically located in such a way that they easily form a circuit of churches in Asia Minor. A messenger could easily deliver a letter to each of the seven churches in order.

From the very beginning of Revelation, we find ourselves living in the tension between heaven and earth. We encounter Christ in a way that we have never seen him before, while at the same time being reminded that we are grounded in our own frail, earthen stories. John experiences this reality as one who shares in the common suffering of humanity and is persecuted for his faithful devotion to Jesus. His exile on the island of Patmos serves as a stark reminder that as followers of Jesus we too are a people of the exile. It is from our own particular islands of exile, among our own communities of faith, and among our own experience of suffering that we stand ready to enter into the apocalyptic world of Revelation.

Behind the Scenes

John's letter to the seven churches begins with these words: "Grace and peace to you from him who is, and who was, and who is to come, and from the seven spirits before his throne, and from Jesus Christ, who is the faithful witness, the firstborn from the dead, and the ruler of the kings of the earth. To him who loves us and has freed us from our sins by his blood and has made us to be a kingdom and priests to serve his God and Father—to him be glory and power for ever and ever! Amen."

While in exile on the island of Patmos, John is in the Spirit on the Lord's Day. He hears behind him the voice like that of a trumpet which instructs him to write on a scroll what he sees and send it to the seven churches of Asia Minor. When he turns to see the voice which is speaking to him, he sees seven golden lampstands and someone like the son of man standing among the lampstands. The one he sees is dressed in a robe that reaches down to his feet and has a golden sash around his chest. His hair is white like wool, as white as snow. His eyes are like blazing fire and his feet are like bronze glowing in a furnace. His voice is like the sound of rushing waters. He holds seven stars in his right hand and a sharp two-edged sword proceeds out of his mouth. His face is like the sun shining in all its brilliance.

When John sees him, he falls at his feet as if he were dead. Placing his right hand on John he says, "Do not be afraid. I am the First and the

Last. I am the Living One; I was dead, and now look, I am alive for ever and ever! And I hold the keys of death and Hades." It is revealed to John that the seven stars are the angels of the seven churches, and the seven lampstands are the seven churches.

To the church at Ephesus, Jesus is the one who holds the seven stars and walks among the seven lampstands. He knows of their good deeds and their lack of tolerance for the wicked. They have endured hardships for the name of Jesus and not grown weary. However, they have forsaken their original love for Jesus. If they do not repent, their lampstand will be removed from them. The one who is victorious will be given the right to eat from the tree of life.

To the church at Smyrna, Jesus is the First and the Last and the one who has died and risen again. Although afflicted and impoverished, they are rich. They will suffer further persecution at the hands of Satan. They are encouraged to be faithful even to death. Those who are will be given life as the victor's crown. Those who are victorious will not be hurt by the second death.

To the church at Pergamum, Jesus is the One with the sharp, double-edged sword proceeding from his mouth. Although Satan has his throne in that city, the followers of Jesus remain true and faithful. However, some hold to the teaching of Balaam and others to the teaching of the Nicolaitans. If they do not repent, Jesus will come and fight against them with the sword of his mouth. Those who are victorious will receive hidden manna and a white stone with a new name written on it, known only to the one who receives it.

To the church at Thyatira, Jesus is the One whose eyes are of blazing fire and his feet of burnished bronze. Jesus knows of their love, deeds, and faith. However, they tolerate Jezebel and are led into sexual immorality and the eating of food offered to idols. Those who do not repent will suffer intensely. Their children will be struck dead. No further burden will be imposed on those who do not follow the teaching of Jezebel and who do not hold to Satan's deep secrets. The one who is victorious will be given authority over the nations. They will also receive the morning star.

To the church at Sardis, Jesus holds the seven spirits of God and the seven stars. Although they have a reputation of being alive, they are in fact dead. If they do not repent and wake up, Jesus will come to them like a thief. Yet, there are a few in Sardis who walk with Jesus and are worthy. Their names will not be blot out from the book of life and they will be acknowledged before the Father and his angels.

To the church at Philadelphia, Jesus is the One is holy and true and holds the key of David. Jesus has placed before them an open door that no one can shut. Although they have little strength, they have kept the word and name of Jesus. Those who are part of the synagogue of Satan will fall down and worship at their feet. Since they have been faithful and have endured, they will be kept from the trial which shall come to the entire world. Those who are victorious will be made pillars in the Temple of God. Jesus will write on them the name of God and the name of the city of God.

Finally, to the church at Laodicea, Jesus is the Amen, the faithful and true witness, and the ruler of God's creation. Jesus knows their deeds, and they are neither cold nor hot. Because they are lukewarm, Jesus will spit them out of his mouth. They do not realize that they are wretched, pitiful, poor, blind, and naked. Jesus stands at their door and knocks. If they open the door, he will come in and eat with them. Those who are victorious will be given the right to sit with Jesus on his throne.

Historical Stage

The opening image of Jesus in Revelation is quite stunning. It consists of a conglomerate of images scattered across various prophets of ancient Israel. In a way that was absolutely unforeseeable, the once isolated and scattered elements come together to form a uniquely cosmic vision of Jesus. Voluminous echoes of Israel's past come gushing forward as John paints this picture of a very apocalyptic Jesus.

This is a great place to see how apocalyptic imagery functions. Nobody would argue that this is what Jesus actually looks like. He only looks this way in this particular apocalyptic casting of him. This is not like a portrait of Jesus that we can hang on the church wall and compare it to the depictions that we are used to seeing – Jesus holding a sheep in his arms, Jesus speaking to a large crowd of people as he prepares to feed them with five loaves and two fishes, Jesus walking on the water in the midst of a storm, Jesus calling Lazarus out from the tomb, Jesus hanging on a cross as he casts his eyes toward heaven, or numerous other depictions of Jesus.

John's cosmic description of Jesus is not intended to be seen as a post-resurrection Jesus that stands in stark contrast to the pre-crucifixion Jesus. Although the various elements used to describe Jesus are not literally real, they point to realities that are literally true. Jesus is not *like* the son of man – he *is* the son of man. Jesus doesn't literally wear a white robe and have a sash around his chest – but he is a priest for all people and in all of his priestly functions he is pure. Jesus does not literally have white hair – but he is eternally wise and fully righteous. The eyes of Jesus don't literally blaze like fire – but he does see into the hearts of all people and into the destiny of the world. His feet are not actually glowing like bronze in a furnace – but he is pure and strong. The actual voice of Jesus does not sound like the indecipherable sound of rushing waters – but he does speak with authority and power. Jesus is not literally walking around holding seven stars in his right hand – but he does reign as king. Jesus does not literally have a two-edged sword proceeding from his mouth – but his very words can heal the sick and raise the dead. Jesus' face does not literally shine like the brilliance of the sun so that no person could ever look at him – but he does fully radiate the love, mercy, and grace of God.

This image of Jesus begs to be let into our imagination. To subject this kind of image of Jesus to our usual tools of analytical and literal interpretation would nearly rise to the level of crucifying him all over again. The opening image of Jesus is not meant to be dissected into small units and parceled out as isolated parts of a much larger vision. This kind of dismembering of Jesus would result in disfigurement and misrepresentation. Jesus is not presented to us in Revelation as an automobile consisting of many parts, but as the cosmic Christ who is fully formed as creator, sustainer, redeemer, and victor.

In the opening scene, Jesus is the revelation of none other than God himself. Or to put it another way, God is fully revealed in Jesus. Jesus is nothing less than the full image of God on cosmic display. This fully orbed Jesus serves as the interpretive image for the entire rest of the story. As the story moves from apocalyptic scene to apocalyptic scene, the cosmic image of Jesus is the thread that runs throughout the various scenes. There are times in Revelation where we will feel the darkness of evil and the weight of suffering that accompanies the clashing of good and evil, the conflict between God and Satan.

Amid all the fury and chaos in Revelation, it would be easy for any of us traveling the seas of this book to lose our complete orientation as the restless waters roll ceaselessly under us and the thick night clouds obscure any hope of navigating the starry heavens. The storms of Revelation are brutal, the clouds dark, the seas volatile. Many readers who have set out to journey the grand narrative of Revelation have never been seen again. They have been swallowed whole by the watery grave of apocalypticism.

The opening image of Jesus as the cosmic Christ is the only way for most of us to start at the beginning of Revelation and have any chance of making it to the very end. We can't simply sail by this image and move on to what's next. We have to enter the image and take it with us through the entirety of our journey. With every turn of the page or shift in scene, we must be able to see the cosmic Christ in all of his fullness, beauty, and power. This vision will be our hope when days of horrific judgment and deep darkness arise and when dragons and beasts emerge from land and sea.

The image of the cosmic Christ serves as an interpretive north star for the entire remainder of Revelation. This star is always ahead of us and is fixed in the skyscape of the story. This is the image which grounds the entire book of Revelation in the reality that Jesus is the triumphant king, the victorious warrior, and the righteous Son of Man. All of these converge in one glorious image as if a whistle had been blown that only the prophets could hear, and the images rush together to form the cosmic Christ.

Christ's activity as king is that of the kind of king who delivers us from our sins by his own blood. His followers are made a kingdom of priests whose purpose is to serve God and give him glory forevermore. This is followed by the promise that he is coming back with clouds and that every eye will see him – even those who had pierced him. These are in essence the words of greeting penned by John as he addresses his audience. It is clear that John is quite aware of the significance and vastness of the redemptive activity of Jesus in terms of his sacrifice and kingship.

It is through the sacrifice of Jesus that God fulfills the promise initially revealed to Moses. Before God revealed the Commandments to Moses at Mount Sinai, he promised that he would create Israel to be a kingdom of priests and a holy nation (Exodus 19:6). The language of Exodus is echoed all throughout Revelation. Just as Israel was beginning a new kind of exile in the wilderness, John was experiencing his own exile on the island of Patmos.

Both the nation of Israel and the community of Christians of John's day were experiencing some form of suffering related to persecution. It is in the context of suffering in which John hears a voice that tells him to write a letter on a scroll to seven churches in Asia Minor. The words to be written would come straight from Jesus himself – the very Jesus who appears to John in all of his glory. This cosmic image of Jesus is critical as the interpretive key to reading the entire story of Revelation. It will be invaluable in unlocking images, visions, and passages that otherwise might be sealed.

The letters that were written to the seven churches are not written as individual letters to be sent separately to each church. All seven letters are included in the one scroll that John writes. The letters do not become private possessions of the seven churches. It is important to keep in mind that the letters to the seven churches are in fact written to the entire church. The message to each of the individual churches is a message to all churches throughout the entire course of church history.

Elements of the cosmic Christ from the opening vision are parceled out to each of the seven churches of Asia Minor. Regardless of what was written to any individual church, Jesus is identified in a particular and unique way to each church. It is from a particular identity that Jesus speaks to the respective churches. To none of the churches does he appear in the complete fulness that he does in the opening cosmic image. This does not suggest that Jesus is not fully present in any of the churches, but rather none of the churches have complete ownership of him or full knowledge of him.

Jesus is fully aware of each church's condition and the element of him that is identified with each church correlates to the condition of that church. When churches are commended, it is because of their faithfulness to Christ and their perseverance during times of persecution and suffering. In cases where Jesus condemns various churches, it is because of errant doctrinal beliefs or immoral practices. In most cases, errant doctrine and immoral practice are intimately connected.

In all cases where correction is needed, there is a call to repentance and a severe consequence if the call to repentance is not heeded. The consequence typically involves a certain kind of judgment of God or the removing of something from the church – in some cases, God's very presence. In cases where the call to repentance is heeded, there is a promise made to the church.

The seven churches each have their own church personalities. Not one of them is a clone of the other. Yet, the cosmic image of Christ relates to each of the churches in a way that is unique to each of them. Although the seven churches are each uniquely different, the message to these churches is applicable to churches of any era, any location, any size, and any church personality style. The basic reality for any church is that no church community is fully formed into the image of Christ. However, Christ is interested in each of his churches and seeks to bring about the full maturity of his body through actions ranging from judgment and discipline to promise and reward.

Contemporary Reflection

In the opening vision of Revelation, we are presented with a clear imaginary depiction of Jesus. Once the image is imprinted in our imagination, we are invited to scan through the seven churches of Asia Minor to see where we might find glimpses of his presence. Although we may see him fully in the opening vision, we only see particular elements of him in each of the churches. As our imagination is unleashed to discover Jesus among the various churches, here are some things that will help us see how the Revelation story speaks to our current imagination as followers of Jesus.

Jesus is present in every church.

It is impossible to have a church without Jesus being present in it. However, it is quite possible to have a religious institution or religious establishment without Jesus. It is even possible to have a building with a steeple, a platform with a pulpit, a communion table with an inscription, and pews with padding, and still have no Jesus sightings. A church is not defined by having all the forms and furniture that we associate with a particular kind of building, but by the living presence of Jesus in the community of those who follow Jesus.

Where there is a congregation where Jesus is not present, it is nothing other than a gathering of people – even if it is a religious gathering. The very existence and nature of a church is defined in terms of Jesus. He is the founder, sustainer, and consummator of the church. As such, he is the Lord and the head of the church. The church is the body of followers through whom the life and mission of Jesus is expressed.

In its expression as the body of Christ, the church is a living organism rather than a religious organization. As in the case of all living organisms there are elements of organization in the church, but the church cannot be reduced to its organizational structure. The sole purpose of the organizational elements or the infrastructure of the church is to serve the purpose of the organism. For example, as human beings we are not identified by our skeletal structure. However, our skeletal structure makes it possible for us to function as humans. Our skeleton serves a much higher purpose than just being a skeleton. When we are reduced to our skeletal structure, we are dead. The same applies to churches. If Jesus is not present, the remaining skeleton of the church does not make up for his absence.

The terms of being a church are actually not complicated. In communities and gatherings where Jesus is present, there is church. In communities and gatherings where Jesus is not present, there is no church. One of the challenges of Revelation to our contemporary context is to offer an honest assessment of the presence of Jesus in our gatherings. Jesus is the one person whose presence is absolutely critical for a church to exist and whose absence makes it impossible for a church to exist at all.

No church can lay claim to the full expression of Jesus.

Even the most hopeful of the seven churches in Revelation could not claim to have the full expression of Jesus as depicted in the opening vision. Each of the churches had a particularly unique way in which they experienced and expressed Jesus. This reality helps us to see that just as living organisms of any species have things which are held in common, they also have distinctions which differentiate them. Dogs share common characteristics that make them dogs, but there are a wide variety of *kinds* of dogs.

The same is true of churches. Although all churches have a Jesus presence in them, no two churches look exactly the same. One of the biggest mistakes that churches are tempted to make is to replicate in their church what they see in another church. This is based on the simple notion that what successfully works in one church will necessarily be successful in another church. This particular mindset is prevalent in church growth models. In these models, "experts" seek to identify what it is that makes a particular church grow. Once they have identified the growth gene, they can then apply it to other churches and wait for the magic to happen.

This assembly line kind of vision can easily strip churches of their particular identity in Christ. The New Testament offers no secret formula for church growth. The letters to the churches serve as reminders that what various congregations are called to be and do should be a direct reflection of how Jesus is uniquely reflected in their particular church. The Jesus gene pool is virtually limitless and the way or combination of ways that Jesus is revealed and manifest in any church are likewise limitless.

There is a very real sense in which every church is incomplete until fully consummated by the full presence of Jesus. Until the moment of consummation, every church has their own limitations in how they experience the presence of Jesus. Even in cases where churches may have a very clear vision of Jesus, the church is only seeing with clarity the part of Jesus that is particularly manifest and made real in their particular community.

The message of Jesus to every church is unique.

Jesus has a message for every congregation in which he is present. Regardless of their spiritual situation, their economic status, their political leaning, or even their false doctrine or immoral behavior, Jesus has something to say to each one of them. Communities that are faithful in their commitment and loyalty to the mission of Jesus are encouraged and commended for their faithfulness. Churches which have lost their spiritual footing and have forsaken their commitment to the confession of Jesus as Lord are harshly rebuked and condemned.

Words of encouragement and rebuke are clearly crafted by Jesus to apply to the unique condition and status of each church. There are no blanket statements for one church that are simply repeated and redelivered to another church. Every word is precise and directed specifically to the church to which Jesus is speaking. The words that he speaks are also a direct reflection of particular elements from the original vision of Jesus. The unique words of Jesus for each church are completely consistent with the unique way that Jesus presents himself to each of the churches.

However, it must not be forgotten that the letters were not written and delivered to each of the seven churches identified. Words of encouragement and rebuke for each of the individual churches were written for the entire church. This serves as a call to all churches where Jesus is present that he has something to say and we have something to hear. Jesus has something to say to every community of followers regardless of who they are, where they gather, or how they practice their faith. However, each community of faith bears the responsibility of recognizing the voice of Jesus and discerning what particular words he has to say to their specific community.

Repentance is as congregational as it is individual.

Repentance is not a word most of us like to hear. When we do hear it, most of us think in terms of sin in our personal lives that needs to be dealt with. We tend to emphasize the need for repentance for those who are coming into initial relationship with God through Jesus. It is a standard part of our evangelical presentation of the gospel. Regardless of your personal view on who is saved and how salvation happens, there is simply no way to avoid the issue of repentance. When Jesus announced at the beginning of his ministry that the Kingdom of God was here, he immediately called for repentance. Prior to the inauguration of Jesus' ministry, John the Baptist was already becoming known for his boldness in naming sin and calling people to repentance.

In the letters to the seven churches, Jesus does not hesitate to call for repentance. This is certainly not surprising given the various kinds of sin represented among the various churches. However, we typically don't consider that the call to repentance in the case of the churches is congregational. Although Jesus may identify certain false beliefs or immoral kinds of behaviors in a particular church, the entire church is called to repentance. The calling of an entire church body to repentance is not unheard of, but it is certainly a rarity for most congregations. Yet, with the churches of Revelation we have clear cases where the entire congregation is called to repentance. A failure to heed the call to repentance results in various forms of punishment.

The very notion that various churches in Revelation are called to repentance is a further reminder that repentance is not just a one and done kind of experience. It is not like going through a door and once through you never have to go through any more doors of repentance as long as you live. The reality is that repentance is more like a road that we travel on for the duration of our lives rather than a door that we go through. There had undoubtedly been acts of initial repentance in the seven churches, otherwise, there would not have even been churches in these particular cities. The message of Jesus to the churches in Revelation is not because they had not stepped through the initial door of repentance, but because they had strayed from the road of repentance in one way or another. Repentance is not just the way *to* life – it is the way *of* life.

Churches must be poised for fresh revelation.

There may be more interpretations of Revelation than we can count, but we would have little disagreement that Revelation is in fact a revelation from God to John. There would also be little disagreement that the central figure of Revelation is clearly Jesus. The revelation concerning what Jesus had to say to each of the seven churches is not only a revelation to John, but a specific revelation aimed for each of the churches. The revelation of Jesus that is depicted in Revelation is quite different from the way that we see Jesus in the Gospels. In the Gospels, Jesus is revealed as the incarnate Son of God who has come to reveal God's love for us and to announce the inauguration of the Kingdom of God. To bring God's redemptive mission to fulfillment, Jesus dies on a cross as he bears our sin and is raised from the grave on the third day and later ascends to the Father.

Although the death, burial, and resurrection of Jesus makes up the heart of the gospel, this is not the way that Jesus is presented in Revelation. Revelation reveals Jesus in an entirely different way. It sees Jesus from a very different perspective than does the Gospels. The focus of Revelation is not on the incarnate Son of God who is sent on a redemptive mission so that we could have a relationship with God. Rather, it is on seeing the consummation of the redemptive mission. We get a peek at what the redemptive mission looks like as it is playing out from the perspective of a world that we otherwise cannot see. It is as if we were totally blind and deaf to the redemptive drama unfolding right behind our eyes and ears. The redemptive mission is truly and really unfolding – we just don't have the capacity to see and hear it apart from revelation given by God.

It is quite obvious that each of the seven churches had some initial spiritual impulse to be able to come together as churches in their respective locations. There was some form of revelation that led to the formation of each church. Most every church throughout the course of Christian history has some founding story that is rooted in the reality that a group of followers of Jesus experienced something that they attribute to God for their formation. It is nearly impossible to imagine the formation of a church without some sort of revelation from God. Even churches that have been formed with less than honest intentions attribute their existence in one way or the other to God.

We can easily grasp the notion that churches have some sort of revelation from God that accounts for their very existence. However, we do not always seem to grasp the reality that churches can only exist as communities of faith when there is receptivity to the ongoing revelation of Jesus in the church. Jesus appeared among the seven churches of Revelation as an ongoing revelation of God. Jesus was compelling the seven churches to embrace revelation that was taking place beyond the original revelation which laid the foundation for the formation of the church. It is this kind of fresh and present revelation that many churches are not experiencing today. Churches often have stories of past revelation from years gone by but often have few stories of fresh revelation from God.

The letters to the seven churches challenge us to be aware and open to the reality that Jesus is the Head of the church and as such has something to say to us. To experience fresh revelation, we must be postured to hear what Jesus is saying to the church. If we are not hearing Jesus, it is not because he has nothing to say – it is because we are not postured to hear what he has to say, or we are not responsive to what he has already said. Receptivity and responsiveness to the current revelation of Jesus is the lifeline for a living community of followers of Jesus.

Wrap Up

In the opening vision of Revelation, Jesus is presented as the cosmic Christ. From the top of his head to the bottom of his feet he is depicted with various apocalyptic images drawn from some of the most apocalyptic passages in the Old Testament. The vision of Jesus positions him in terms of how he relates to the past, the present, and the future. It also positions him as he relates to the Godhead on the one hand and to the earthly churches on the other. Various elements relate to various functions such as king, priest, and servant.

Before pressing forward to the story of redemption that is beyond our earthly purview, we are first introduced to the stories of seven churches throughout Asia Minor. These stories are local and historical. They each have their own particular vision of Jesus and each of them are the recipients of the words of the cosmic Christ. None of the churches are totally perfect but all of them are living communities where Christ is or has been present. Words of both commendation and condemnation are spoken by Jesus to the various churches. The goal for each of the churches is the same – that through their continuing or renewed commitment to Jesus they will be victorious.

The image of the cosmic Christ and his speaking to each of the churches invites us immediately into the world of imagination. Even though the churches themselves are local and historical, the presence of Jesus among them is mystical and mysterious. It is not possible to see the cosmic Christ or to hear his message to the churches without an imagination that is both strongly robust and gently fertile. The gateway to Revelation is something like the gate that leads to eternal life – it is narrow on the approach but broad on the exit. Jesus is the narrow way to life but the life to which he leads us expands beyond creation itself.

The journey ahead simply cannot be taken without the full engagement of our imagination. As we experience Jesus in terms of the cosmic Christ who speaks to his people, we are already well beyond the limits which reason and analysis can offer to us – even at their very best. Our imagination allows us to see and hear what we otherwise could not see or hear. It invites us to a journey which we could not otherwise take.

It challenges us to a transformation that we otherwise could not experience. For this journey, let's lay aside our usual confidence in reason and let something new and unreasonable take place in us.

ReImagine

The book of Revelation is revealed to John who is in exile on the island of Patmos. He has also endured some form of suffering for his faith. The theme of exile is common throughout the Bible. Israel was in exile in Egypt and then again years later in Babylon. Many of the prophets lived in some form of exile. Even the church is considered to be a people of exile. Reflect on how you and your community of faith are exiles. In what ways does this reality shape your approach to engaging Revelation?

Although the cosmic Christ in the opening vision is presented as a composite, yet complete, picture of Jesus, he is only partially present in each of the seven churches of Asia Minor. In what ways does this help shape our own understanding of the presence of Jesus in our personal lives and in the life of our faith community?

Just as Christ had something to say to each of the seven churches then, he has something to say to each of his churches today. Think about some of the ways that we hear him in our own faith communities. What kinds of things is he saying to you and your faith community specifically? What images of Jesus are most prevalent in your community of faith?

We tend to have a short-sighted vision of repentance in many of our faith communities. Although we understand the significance of repentance in the role that it plays in coming into a relationship with God, we often fail to realize that repentance is a lifelong experience. We also tend to fail to realize that repentance is not just a personal experience, it is a corporate experience. Consider ways that your community of faith might need to practice corporate repentance.

Second Image:
The Slain Lamb

Our imagination is stretched to the utmost, not, as in fiction, to imagine things which are not really there, but just to comprehend those things which 'are' there.
Richard Feynman

The image of Jesus in this second vision is vastly different than the cosmic Christ vision encountered in the opening scene of Revelation. Whereas the former vision of Jesus is one in which the various elements are designed to evoke a vision of the glorious and the victorious Christ, this vision speaks to the crucified and sacrificial Christ. Whereas the very exalted Christ appears in the very earthly churches of Asia Minor, the Christ as the sacrificial Lamb appears in the exalted courts of the throne room of God.

The shift in scenery is quite stark and very sudden. Immediately after the letters to the seven churches of Asia Minor, John looks and sees an open door in heaven. A voice like a trumpet calls John to come through the door where he will be shown things that will happen next. The voice that sounds like a trumpet is none other than the voice of God inviting John to enter through the open door.

A common feature in apocalyptic writings is that of an individual being transported through a portal to a different world. In this case, John is transported from his place of exile on Patmos to a heavenly throne room scene. Some interpreters see this event as a kind of rapture of the church. However, the book of Revelation itself does not contain the notion of a rapture. This is simply a feature of apocalyptic literature and is not intended in any way to suggest a rapture of any sort. John's transport to the throne room is so that John can have access to the drama which is unfolding behind the scenes of what is taking place in the historical setting.

At the very center of the throne room scene is the One who sits on the throne and to whom all of heaven's worship is directed. Yet, none of heaven's beings are worthy to open the scroll in God's hand. Our imagination gets pressed to the limit when it is revealed that only the sacrificial Lamb can take the scroll to break the seals and reveal its contents. As such, the worship that focused on the One on the throne is now directed toward the Lamb who takes the scroll and opens its contents.

Behind the Scenes

After John writes the letters to the seven churches as God instructs him, he then sees an open door to heaven. A voice like the sound of a trumpet invites him to come and see what things will happen next. John is immediately in the Spirit and sees a throne with someone sitting on it. The one sitting on the throne has the appearance of jasper and ruby. A rainbow encircles the throne and shines like an emerald. Twenty-four thrones with an elder on each throne surrounds the throne. The elders are dressed in white and have crowns of gold on their heads. Flashes of lightning and peals of thunder proceed from the throne. In front of the throne are seven lamps which are the seven spirits of God. In front of the throne is a sea of glass as clear as crystal.

Around the throne in the center are four living creatures covered with eyes on the front and back. The first living creature is like a lion, the second like an ox, the third has the face of a man, and the fourth is like a flying eagle. Each of the four creatures also have six wings covered with eyes. Day and night, the creatures proclaim, "Holy, holy, holy, is the Lord God Almighty, who was, and is, and is to come." Whenever the creatures give glory to God, the twenty-four elders fall down before the one who sits on the throne and worship. As they lay their crowns before the one who sits on the throne, they declare, "You are worthy, our Lord and God, to receive glory and honor and power, for you created all things."

    John then sees in the right hand of the one who sits on the throne a scroll with writing on both sides and sealed with seven seals. A mighty angel asks if anyone is worthy to break the seals and open the scroll. John weeps as no one in heaven or on earth is found worthy to open the seals and read the scroll. An elder tells John not to weep for the Lion of the tribe of Judah, the Root of David has triumphed and is worthy to open the seals and read the scroll.

    John then sees a Lamb as if it had been slain standing at the center of the throne. The Lamb has seven horns and seven eyes, which are the seven spirits of God sent out into all the earth. When the Lamb takes the scroll, the four living creatures and the twenty-four elders fall down before the Lamb. Each of them has a harp and are holding golden bowls of incense, which are the prayers of God's people. They sing a new song, "You are worthy to take the scroll and open its seals, because you were slain, and with your blood you purchased for God persons of every tribe and language and people and nation. You have made them to be a kingdom of priests to serve our God, and they will reign on the earth."

    John then sees multitudes of angels – thousands upon thousands, and ten thousand times ten thousand. They encircle the throne and declare, "Worthy is the Lamb who was slain, to receive power and wealth and wisdom and strength and honor and glory and praise." The declaration is made by every creature in heaven, on earth, under the earth, and under the sea. The four living creatures declare "Amen" and the twenty-four elders fall down and worship.

Historical Stage

When John goes through the open door he finds himself in the midst of a majestic throne room scene. Although it is clear that the person sitting on the throne is God, it is never stated as such. John simply describes his experience of being immediately in the Spirit and seeing the throne with someone sitting on it. John leaves the description of the One who sits on the throne to the imagination. There is no attempt to try to depict God in any other terms than that of finest gems and stones. Undoubtedly, any depiction or description of God would fall woefully short in capturing his glory and majesty. God does not consist of jasper and ruby – they simply denote in earthly ways the glorious appearance of God.

From the throne comes flashes of lightning along with rumblings and peals of thunder. These images recall the dramatic presence of God at various junctures in Israel's history. After Moses led the Hebrews through the Red Sea, they came to the foot of Mount Sinai three months later. When God descended on the mountain there was thunder and lightning with a thick cloud over the mountain. There was also a loud trumpet blast, and the mountain trembled.

The lightening, thunder, smoke, and trembling that occurred as God descended on Mount Sinai not only depicted God's presence on the mountain, it was also a sign to the Hebrews that anybody who touched the mountain would die. Moses alone was allowed to go up the mountain without being struck down in death. The thunder and lightning that John sees and hears recalls God's revelation of himself on Mount Sinai. The God who once used a mountain as his earthly throne is the God that sits on heaven's throne.

In front of the throne John sees what he describes as a sea of glass, clear as crystal. In contrast to the many images of seas raging in tumultuous fits of waves on the surface, threatening storm clouds overhead, uncontrollable winds all around, and dangerous monsters beneath the waters, the sea in front of the throne is calm, the water is clear, and there are no dangerous monsters lurking underneath. The throne of God is in no danger of succumbing to the powerful and deadly forces often encountered on the open seas. In fact, the sea in front of the throne appears to be in total submission to the One who sits on the throne.

Also in front of the throne are seven blazing lamps representing the seven spirits of God. This does not literally mean that there are seven different spirits – there is only one Spirit. The use of the number seven as used in apocalyptic literature refers to the fullness and completeness of something. Here it refers to the reality that the Spirit of God is present in fullness. The fire recalls God's presence in such events as the ceremonial establishing of the covenant with Abraham, God's leading of the Israelites in the wilderness by night, the encounter of Moses with God at the burning bush, and the appearance of tongues of fire on the one hundred and twenty disciples gathered in a room for prayer on the day of Pentecost.

John further sees a rainbow shining like an emerald that encircles the throne. The rainbow invites us to extend our imagination all the way back to the days of Noah. After the great flood washed over the earth, the appearance of the rainbow in the sky was given as a sign that God would never again destroy the earth by flood. This sign of promise and hope which was given to Noah is now used as an image that the One who sits on the throne is a keeper of promises and a conveyor of hope. The crystal sea in front of the throne lies in submission and poses no threat to heaven's inhabitants even as flashes of lightning and peals of thunder proceed from the throne.

This amazing collection of images can only be entertained in the imagination. These are not literal descriptions of God on his throne. To literalize the vision would only serve to limit our vision of God on his heavenly throne amid the heavenly court. Only through the portal of our imagination do we have access to the throne room and begin to see the One who sits on the throne and to hear the voice of the One who speaks creation into existence.

John describes several circles of heavenly beings that surround the throne. The four living creatures that John sees are somewhat similar to the four living creatures that Ezekiel saw in a vision as he was sitting by the Kebar River while in exile in Babylon. In Ezekiel's vision the heavens open up and he sees an immense cloud with flashes of lightning and surrounded by brilliant light. The center of the fire is like glowing metal and in the fire he sees four living creatures. However, the four living creatures that Ezekiel sees all have the form of a human, but each has four faces and four wings. Each of the four creatures have the face of a human, a face of a lion on the right side, a face of an ox on the left side, and a face of an eagle.

Regardless of the similarities and differences between the four creatures that Ezekiel saw and the four that John sees, it is clear that they are intended to imaginatively represent various orders of living beings on the earth. The lion, the ox, the human, and the eagle represent the highest order of beings in their respective species. Their sole function in this throne room scene is to declare without ceasing the holiness of God – "Holy, holy, holy is the Lord God Almighty, who was, and is, and is to come."

Beyond the inner circle of the four living creatures is the circle consisting of twenty-four elders who sit on twenty-four thrones. The elders are dressed in white and have crowns of gold on their heads. Their white robes are indicative of priestly functions, and the golden crowns are indicative of their kingly roles. It is not specifically stated what significance is to be attached to the number twenty-four. Regardless of the meaning of the number, the role of the twenty-four elders is quite clear. Whenever the living creatures give honor, glory, and thanks to the One who sits on the throne, the twenty-four elders fall down before him and worship.

Our imagination allows us to hear this majestic antiphonal praise which constantly fills the throne room and beyond. The four living creatures proclaim the holiness of God and in response the twenty-four elders declare the worthiness of God. The sights and sounds of the heavenly vision are beyond description. They are certainly far more glorious and majestic than anyone or anything associated with the Roman imperial court. The glory of the Roman emperor with all of his attendants comes nowhere close to what John sees in heaven's throne room.

John then sees the One who is seated on the throne holding a scroll in his right hand. The scroll has writing on both the inside and the outside and is sealed with seven seals. John's weeping at the prospect that there was no one among the four living creatures, the twenty-four elders, and the countless numbers of angels who could take the scroll and open its contents is quite understandable.

The scroll contains the full story of God's Kingdom – a story that will never be read because it is sealed. It is not only sealed with one seal as would be customary in the correspondence of a king or dignitary, but with seven seals. John could only imagine what story might have been told in the scroll – a story that would be eternally untold. Undoubtedly, John must have hoped that one of the four creatures before the throne, or one of the twenty-four elders surrounding the throne would surely be worthy candidates to come forward and take the scroll and break the seals. How could it be possible that not a single one of them was worthy to approach the throne and receive the scroll? In this very moment itself, it certainly must have seemed to John that the story of God would remain a mystery for all the ages.

In that very moment, one of the elders tells John not to weep for the Lion of the tribe of Judah, the root of David, has triumphed and is worthy to break the seven seals and open the scroll. A new creature that John has not yet seen stands at the center of the throne – a Lamb that appears to have been slain. The Lamb has seven horns and seven eyes, which are the seven spirits that God has sent out unto the earth. The imaging here is quite remarkable. The elder says there is a Lion, but when John looks, he sees a Lamb – a sacrificed one at that. However, this was not a sacrificial lamb that had been drained of its life but one that was fully alive.

When the Lamb takes the scroll from the One sitting on the throne, the four creatures and the twenty-four elders fall down before the Lamb and sing a new song. In this highly imaginative scene, the worship of all of heaven's creatures is redirected toward the Lamb. The worship that has been reserved only for the One on the throne in the previous scene is now lavishly poured out before the Lamb encircled by the living creatures and the twenty-four elders. The worship directed toward the One who sits on the throne focused on eternal essence and creation. In contrast, the worship directed toward the Lamb focuses on the act of sacrifice and the redemption of all people.

With only a modest amount of imagination, it is not difficult to see the connection between the slain Lamb here and the slain lamb whose blood was placed on the doorposts of the Hebrew children on the night that the death angel passed over them. The slain Lamb of Revelation takes us back to the greatest redemptive act of the Old Testament – nothing other than the exodus from Egypt. This Lamb, however, is the leader of a new and greater exodus. Unlike the Hebrews who were rescued from their Egyptian oppressors, the redemption associated with the slain Lamb is of a higher order. It is not a rescue on dry land as the waters stand aside like large towers of protection, but one that involves a greater kind of sacrifice in the face of a greater kind of enemy and results in a greater kind of redemption.

The new song of the four creatures and the twenty-four elders also casts our imagination back to God speaking to Moses from Mount Sinai instructing him what to say to the people. Moses is to remind the people that they have seen God's deliverance and how he has carried them on eagle's wings and brought them to himself. If they keep God's covenant, they would be a treasured possession and would be a kingdom of priests and a holy nation. The new song of redemption furthermore suggests that a new people would make up the Kingdom and would serve the role as God's priest on the earth. The innumerable hosts of angels join in the new song. All creatures in heaven, on earth, and in the sea join in. The four living creatures before the throne offer a benedictory "Amen" and the twenty-four elders fall down and worship.

John's entrance through the door leading to a vision of the throne room is awe inspiring to say the least. The breathtaking experience of being in the throne room simply cannot be described in literal terms with propositional truths. His vision is one that can only be experienced in terms of the most apocalyptic language that is available to him. John is not giving an analysis of the vision that he sees. The vision is not subject to our powers of reason and rationality. He is painting a picture inasmuch as language will allow and is inviting us to embrace it with our imagination.

The vision of the slain Lamb is the climax of the throne room vision. In the first scene the vision of Jesus is cast first and the letters to the seven churches are written in light of the presence of the cosmic Christ among the earthly churches. In this scene all of the astounding images come first, and the sacrificial Lamb takes the stage once all of the heavenly props are in place. It is something of a grand scheme set up. When John sees the throne where the One sits among the four creatures and twenty-four elders, it could be easily assumed that he had encountered the main attraction.

However, as the scene unfolds, it becomes clear that the main event shifts from the One sitting on the throne to the sacrificial Lamb. It is not until the appearance of the sacrificial Lamb that there is any hint of the innumerable hosts of angels who join in the praise, and that furthermore all creatures in heaven, on the earth, and in the sea also render their voices of praise to the Lamb. The worship that takes place when the sacrificial Lamb is revealed appears to be even broader and deeper than the worship prior to his appearing. It is only when the sacrificial Lamb appears that the elders are said to have harps and golden bowls of incense. It is only after the vision of the sacrificial Lamb that we hear of the prayers of God's people and the singing of a new song.

The majesty of this heavenly portrait of the throne room leaves no way for John to have been prepared for the appearance of a slain Lamb in the midst of such a glorious and holy scene. The appearance of such a being does not seem to readily fit the scene given everything else that John describes in the vision. At first glance, it seems that the slain Lamb plays the role of an anti-hero. The sight of blood against the backdrop of such a pristine and perfectly ordered throne room is difficult to hold in tension.

Yet, it is this very slain Lamb that becomes the focal point of the heavenly scene. All worship and praise are now directed to the slain Lamb and the worshippers are extended beyond even those of the opening throne room scene. John offers no theological explanation for why there is a Lamb and why it bears the marks of having been slain. Neither does he offer any explanation as to how the Lamb that was slain is now fully alive.

Although there are no explanations as to the story associated with the slain Lamb, it is clear that all of heaven and earth are swept together into a grand symphony of praise that is a response to the very fact that the Lamb is slain. The response is spontaneous and so splendid that all that is left to do by the twenty-four elders is to fall down and worship and all that is left to say by the fours creatures is "Amen!"

Contemporary Reflection

John's journey through the portal from earth to heaven leads him right into the throne room itself. There is no way that John could have ever imagined that in one moment he would be writing letters to the seven churches of Asia Minor and in another moment he would be witnessing the majestic wonder of worship as it unfolds in heaven. In contrast to the very earthly and even fragile state of the churches on earth, his experience of the throne room is filled with images and beings that he had never seen proclaiming words of praise that he had never heard. Here are some basic reflections about worship that emerge out of the heavenly vision.

Worship is the first and foremost activity of creation.

As John arrives in the throne room it is obvious that worship is the activity that is taking place. It is not taking place as one of a number of activities that takes place in heaven, it is taking place as *the* activity that takes place in heaven. There is no sense that there was a starting point at which worship began and that there would ever be an ending point where worship reaches its final crescendo.

The heavenly scene of worship serves as a model for the earthly church. The first and foremost activity of the church is that it is a worshipping community. The worship of the church is not confined to worship services. Rather, worship is the *way* that the church lives out its life in every single moment of every single day. This is the worship that happens with every breath that we take. When worship is embraced as the very essence of our activity and being, the smallest and most menial of activities can be filled with the breath of heaven.

It is easy for churches to become so activity oriented that they lose sight of their primary calling to be worshipping communities. The greatest challenge for nearly every church is that we have relegated worship to be a *part* of what we do rather than the *whole* of who we are. It simply comes down to nothing other than the fact that in our prevailing images of churches as institutions and organizations, we for the most part have a half-stunted theology and practice of worship.

Unlike John's full orbed vision of worship as he stands in the throne room, our vision of worship tends to extend no further than the dimensions of our sanctuary space. Our vision of worship can even be neatly packaged into an order of worship which takes place at a scheduled time and place. There is certainly nothing wrong with having corporate worship at specific times and places that follow a particular order or flow of worship. In fact, we are commanded to engage in such gatherings for the expressed purpose of worship.

Our short-sightedness concerning worship can be seen when we think of worship as an event that takes place at the church at a certain time rather than a lifestyle that is ingrained in us for every moment of every day. Worship is not something that we come to and leave, it is something that flows through us always. At the end of the day, worship is how we are oriented toward God. What John witnessed in the throne room scene was that every creature was oriented towards the throne. It did not matter whether they were in the most inner circle of creatures or the most outer edges of beings.

Not only is every creature in heaven oriented toward the throne, their entire reason for being is to worship the One on the throne. They exist for no other purpose than to engage in the ceaseless activity of worship. It was not just the first thing they did, or even the foremost thing they did – it was everything they did.

Worship is the most pervasive activity in the world.

Worship is not a strictly religious activity – it is a pervasive activity that takes place in all realms of life at all times. Worship is assigning supreme worth to someone or something. As such, every person of every color, creed, and nationality is involved in the ongoing activity of worship. In this sense, worship is not even confined to religious faiths and practices. It is simply a recognition that our faith and practices follow whatever or whoever it is that we assign the most worth to. Our highest value is that which we worship. For example, if the greatest value in our life is to be wealthy, we will worship wealth. The same holds true for any other thing or person that we embrace as having greatest worth.

The uniqueness of Christianity is that Christ is held forth as holding the highest worth. As such, he is worthy of being praised and worshipped. The appearance of the slain Lamb at the middle of the throne immediately compels the worship of every being in heaven and on earth. Even with all of the good things that God has created, none of them rival the worship of the Lamb. Nothing in the heavens or under the heavens commands the worship that the Lamb does.

Although the Lamb is the one in Revelation who is worthy of the worship of all beings, not everyone worships the Lamb. Although the slain Lamb possesses the full sovereignty of God, he exercises his sovereignty in such a way as to give us freedom as to how we will respond to his worth. Those who ascribe supreme worth to anything or anyone other than the Lamb are destined to wherever their worship will take them.

The ultimate issue of worship is whether the person or thing that we worship is fully capable of delivering on the promise that it offers. Every one of us is banking on some fulfillment that what we hold as worth will deliver. The promises of other things or persons to worship loom large, but the payoffs are consistently far less than the promises that are made. Only in the case of the slain Lamb does the promise of life and the fulfillment of that promise come to full realization.

Worship is the context of Revelation.

John's apocalyptic journey from one world to another world lands him right in the middle of an amazing and breathtaking worship scene. This scene is the first vision that John has that is beyond his earthly experience. The transition between letters to seven churches in Asia Minor to the very throne room of God is by any measure a very significant transition.

Not only is the transition quite significant, the vision of Christ in each setting is lightyears apart. The cosmic Christ of the initial vision of Revelation is nowhere to be seen in the heavenly throne vision. There would have been little surprise if the cosmic Christ had been the one who stepped forward to take the scroll from the hand of the One who sat on the throne. It would have made perfect sense for the cosmic Christ to then begin to break the seals and open the scroll to unfurl the story which would otherwise be forever sealed.

However, this is not at all the way that Christ is revealed in the throne scene. There would have been no possible way for John to foresee that the one who would step forward and take the scroll and open its seals was a Lamb that had been slain and yet was still alive. It would have seemed under the circumstances that if anyone could take the scroll it would have been none other than the cosmic Christ – certainly not a slain Lamb. Given the kind of death that Jesus suffered on the earth, it would have perhaps seemed more natural that his presence in each of the seven churches of Asia Minor would have been in terms of that of being the slain Lamb.

As it turns out, it is the slain Lamb who appears in the throne room. As it further turns out, it is the slain Lamb who becomes the clear center of attention and who is the object of worship of the four living creatures, the twenty-four elders, myriads of angelic hosts, and all creatures of the earth and sea. Not only would there have been no surprise to have seen the cosmic Christ in the middle of the throne, there would have been little surprise for all creatures in heaven and earth to worship the cosmic Christ standing in supreme glory at the very center of heaven's throne.

Just as the cosmic Christ serves as an interpretive key for reading the entire apocalyptic story of Revelation, the throne room serves as the context for reading the story. The book of Revelation is written *from* the perspective of worship *for* the worshipping community. It was not written for the sake of timelines or millennial options or signs of the times. It was written for the sole sake of worship. Everything that happens in the throne scene is oriented around worship. The throne room scene functions to set the entire book of Revelation in the context of a community who worships the slain Lamb. Both the grand and gross images of the apocalyptic story of Revelation seek to compel and invite the readers to use their imagination to enter into the mysterious and transforming act of worship.

The worship of Christ is an act of subterfuge.

Much has been made of the fact that the One who appears in the middle of the throne to take the scroll and open the seals is a slain Lamb. The image of a slain Lamb hardly speaks to the notion of a triumphant and victorious conqueror. Yet, at the very heart of the redemptive act of God in the world there is a sacrificial Lamb who is the Lion from the tribe of Judah. In great contrast to the more kingly tones and images that characterize the throne room, the image of a slain Lamb runs counter to our instincts and expectations.

There are no thrones, crowns, robes, scepters, statues, coins, armies or attendants associated with slain lambs. There is no sense in which slain lambs have ever been worshipped, idolized, or thought of as depicting strength and power. If anything, slain lambs are typically associated with such things as meekness, weakness, defenselessness, and helplessness. There is no sense of glory or majesty associated with the sacrificing of a lamb. Perhaps there is some possible sense of glory or majesty that could be associated with the sacrifice of a bull – but certainly not with a lamb.

Although the offering of lambs as sacrifices were a staple of Israel's worship practices, it was never the lambs themselves which were the objects of worship. They were simply the offerings and sacrifices that were rendered to God during the act of worship. However, the slain Lamb that is alive becomes the focal point of worship in the throne room scene. Just as it goes against our sensibilities that it is a slain Lamb that is the only one who is worthy to take the scroll and open its contents, so does it go against our sensibilities that it is the slain Lamb who is the object of worship for all creatures and all creation.

Christian worship is an act of the greatest subterfuge ever because of precisely this – at the heart of our worship is a slain Lamb who lives. The very idea of such a thing overthrows the entire ordered universe with all of its power structures. In what world would a sacrificial lamb ever emerge as the highest possible being that commands the worship of the entire world? Yet, it is this very reality that is the signature stamp par excellence of the Christian faith.

As a people who worship the slain Lamb, our very act of worship undermines and overthrows the powers that seek to hold us captive to sin, death, and hell. Our deliverance does not come by military force, political power, or economic strength. It comes by the power of the Lamb that was slain and risen on the third day. The victory cannot be separated from the suffering, pain, agony, humiliation, and death of the Lamb. As worshippers of the Lamb, our very worship turns the powers of this world upside down.

Worship generates more worship.

Worship is the single most significant act that we participate in. It is the one act which orients every single thing in the universe. As we worship we are drawn into an experience where we see everything from a new perspective. We see the majestic throne room of God and how all of creation relates to the One sitting on the throne and the Lamb. The vision of worship encompasses everything from heaven to earth. There is no part of creation which falls beyond the pale of worship.

As we have seen earlier, worship cannot be restricted to a church activity that happens at such a place at such a time. Worship permeates the very fabric of existence and essence. As John stands in the throne room, he gets a firsthand glimpse of the power, beauty, and pervasiveness of worship. He sees how absolutely essential worship is to not just all of heaven's beings but to every part of creation. He also hears the declarations and proclamations which accompany the acts of worship. The words he hears are filled with praise for the One who sits on the throne and for the living slain Lamb.

It is quite clear that the acts and words of worship witnessed by John are unceasing. In one sense the scene depicts something of a worship loop. However, it is not a loop which is nothing more than a replay of what has gone before, it is the kind of loop in which every measure of worship generates a deeper depth, a greater height, a broader range. Worship is a dynamic experience, not a static experience. It has rise and fall, ebb and flow, movement and motion. Every act and expression of worship generates even fuller and greater worship.

When the book of Revelation is read and experienced in the context of worship, it too takes on a particular kind of life that is self-generating. Its message does not consist of a static litany of theological truths and propositions. Rather, Revelation is a living and breathing book which has a dynamism all of its own. It cannot be confined, contained, restricted, or managed by our fanciful schemes of timelines, events, identity of particular persons, or millennial options. Each one of these attempts to subdue Revelation only leaves us with an emptiness that we had hoped could be filled with such machinations and manipulations of the text.

Engaging Revelation as worshippers and worshipping communities invites us to set our sails high and let the winds of worship take us wherever they will. The journey is forever ongoing, the experience is always new and fresh, and the more our sails are positioned for worship, the greater and fuller our worship will always become.

Wrap Up

A majestic and glorious throne room scene is the most unlikely place where we might expect to see a lamb. The other creatures surrounding the throne are described in terms of splendor, power, and strength. The appearance of a lion would not at all be shocking. But the vision of a Lamb as if it had been slain but is still living is shockingly out of place and totally unforeseeable. Nevertheless, it is precisely what John sees.

Not only is the vision of a slain Lamb totally unexpected, the activity of such a Lamb is even more unexpected. Of all of heaven's creatures in all of their splendor, not a single one of them is able to step forward and take the scroll of God from his hand. Only the Lamb is worthy to do so – a Lamb that still bears the blood stain marks of sacrifice.

Once the Lamb steps forward to take the scroll, the entire focus of worship shifts to the Lamb. The Lamb is not just the description of another heavenly being surrounding the throne of God who engages in worship of the One who sits on the throne. Rather, the Lamb is at throne and receives the full worship of all of heaven's creatures. The worship that had been given to the One who sits on the throne focused on the reality that he had created all things. When the Lamb enters the scene and takes the scroll, the worship of the Lamb focuses on the sacrificial act of the Lamb.

The scene of the slain Lamb standing at the throne of God is vastly different than the previous vision of the Christ in which John saw him in cosmic splendor on the earth. It would have been far more understandable if when John turned to see who could take the scroll and open its seals if the same Christ he had previously seen was the one that he now sees standing before the throne.

Once the shocking and surprising terms of worship are established, the story can move forward. In the upcoming judgments of the seals, trumpets, and bowls, there will be the unmistakably clear sense that the slain Lamb is intimately involved in all that happens. We might not always see him, but we will know that he is present, and we will feel his presence not only in the throne room as John did, but on the stage of history as the events begin to unfold. As the story is told, we too will be drawn to worship the Lamb that was slain yet lives.

ReImagine

The two opening depictions of Jesus are a story of contrasts. The first image is of the cosmic Christ among the earthly churches of Asia Minor and the second image is the sacrificial Lamb standing at the throne of God. We would have expected just the opposite – the sacrificial Lamb among the churches and the cosmic Christ at the throne of God. Reflect on ways that these two very different visions of Christ in two very different places might serve to shape a new vision of *how* and *where* we see Jesus.

The act of worship is the primary purpose of our lives and the primary function of the church. Consider how the worship scene functions in the book of Revelation. In what ways does the worship scene set the stage and prepare our hearts for the heavy lifting of Revelation which is yet to come?

John's vision of a sacrificial Lamb that yet lives is quite stunning. Even more stunning is the fact that of all of the creatures and beings in heaven, the sacrificial Lamb is the only one who can take the scroll from the hand of God and break its seven seals. Reflect on how this one act impacts the rest of Revelation. Reflect on ways that the sacrificial Lamb relates to the entire unfolding of human history.

Third Image:
The Judging Lamb

Imagination is the only weapon in the war against reality.
Lewis Carroll

The judgments of God and of the Lamb take place in a series of judgments that feature the breaking of seals, the blowing of trumpets, and the pouring out of bowls. In each cycle there are seven judgments. As the judgments progress from one cycle to the next, there is also an increased intensity of judgment. The final series consisting of the seven bowls of judgment represent the finality and totality of God's judgment.

The cycles of judgment are spread out among ten chapters in Revelation. However, they are not told with seamless continuity as they move through the cycles. As we shall see in the next chapter, there are powerful images of God's protection and salvation of his people in the so-called "interlude" sections. During the interludes, judgment is held at bay while visions of protection and salvation are recorded.

The judgments themselves are dramatic, vivid, intense, destructive, and cosmic – just to use a few words to describe them. The only means by which such horrendous judgements can be depicted is through the use of apocalyptic language. It must be kept in mind that the apocalyptic language which carries the freight of judgment is intentionally non-literal. Apocalyptic language is a literary tool which allows for the kinds of descriptions and depictions that are about to follow. Although judgment is quite literal and is very real, the language of apocalypse which conveys the judgments is not intended to convey the judgments in a literal form. This in no way diminishes the historical reality of punishment – it simply describes punishment in terms that allow us to imagine the larger powers at play which are beyond historical horizons.

Behind the Scenes

As the Lamb opens the first seal, John sees a white horse. With a bow in his hand and a crown on his head, its rider goes out to conquer. When the Lamb opens the second seal a fiery red horse appears. Its rider wields a great sword and is given power to take peace from the earth and to make people kill each other. After the third seal is opened, John sees a black horse with a rider who holds a pair of scales in his hands. One of the four living creatures proclaims, "Two pounds of wheat for a day's wages, and six pounds of barley for a day's wages, and do not damage the oil and the wine." When the Lamb opens the fourth seal, a pale horse appears and its rider is named Death, and Hades is following close behind.

When the Lamb opens the fifth seal, John sees the souls under the altar of those who have been slain because of the word of God and their testimony. With a loud voice the souls call out, "How long, Sovereign Lord, holy and true, until you judge the inhabitants of the earth and avenge our blood?" Each of the souls is given a white robe and told to wait a little longer until the full number of their brothers and sisters are killed.

The opening of the sixth seal results in a great earthquake. The sun turns black like sackcloth and the moon turns blood red. The stars in the sky fall to the earth as figs drop from a tree. The heavens recede like a scroll being rolled up. and every mountain and island is displaced. Everyone from rulers to slaves and from wealthy to poor, seek refuge in caves and among the rocks of the mountains. They call out to the mountains and rocks to fall on them and hide them from the face of him who sits on the throne and from the wrath of the Lamb.

There are two major "interludes" in this section. The first follows the opening of the sixth seal and the second follows the opening of the sixth trumpet. Both interludes consists of visions which depict God's protection and salvation of his people. These particular visions will be dealt with in the next chapter.

When the Lamb opens the seventh seal, there is silence in heaven for about half an hour. Seven angels standing before God are given seven trumpets. Another angel with a golden censer comes and stands at the golden altar before the throne of God. The angel is given much incense to offer with the prayers of all God's people. The smoke of the incense mixed together with the prayers of God's people goes up from the angel's hand to God. The angel then takes the censer and fills it with fire from the altar and hurls it to the earth. There are peals of thunder, rumblings, flashes of lightning and an earthquake.

With the blowing of the first trumpet, hail and fire mixed with blood are hurled down on the earth. This is very different from the censer filled with fire that the angel hurled down to the earth. As a result of the judgment associated with the first trumpet, one-third of the earth is burned up, a third of all trees are burned up, and all the green grass is burned up. With the blast of the second trumpet, something like a huge mountain ablaze with fire is thrown into the sea. A third of the sea turns to blood and a third of all sea creatures die and a third of all ships are destroyed.

When the third angel blows his trumpet, a star named Wormwood falls from the sky on a third of all rivers and springs of water. A third of the waters turns bitter and many people die from the waters. When the fourth angel blows his trumpet, a third of the sun, moon, and stars are struck and are turned dark. A third of the day and a third of the night are without light. John then hears an eagle flying through mid-air proclaiming "Woes" to the inhabitants of the earth with the blowing of the three trumpets yet to come.

At the blowing of the fifth trumpet a star that had fallen from the sky to the earth is given the key to the shaft of the Abyss. Great smoke arises from the Abyss when it is opened, and the sun and sky are darkened. Locusts come down on the earth from the smoke of the Abyss and are given power like that of scorpions. The locusts are told to not harm the earth, but only those who do not have the seal of God on their foreheads. They are further told not to kill people, but they are allowed to torture them for five months. The agony of those stung by scorpions would be so great that they would seek their own deaths, but their attempts at death would end in failure.

The locusts look like horses prepared for battle. They wear on their heads what appears to be crowns of gold and they have faces like humans. Their hair is like that of a woman's and their teeth are like those of lions. Their breastplates are like that of iron and the thunderous sound of their wings is like that of horses and chariots rushing into battle. In their tails are stingers with which they could torture people for five months. They have as king over them the angel of the Abyss.

At the blowing of the sixth trumpet, John hears a voice coming from the four corners of the golden altar located before the throne of God. It tells the sixth angel to release the four angels who are bound at the Euphrates. The four angels are released to kill a third of all mankind. The horses and riders have a breastplate of fiery red, dark blue, and yellow sulfur. A third of mankind is killed by the plagues of fire, smoke, and sulfur that come out of their mouths. Their tails are like snakes having heads with which they can inflict injury. Those who are not killed refuse to repent from their various sins.

With the sounding of the seventh trumpet, voices in heaven declare that the kingdom of the Messiah has come and he would reign forever. The twenty-four elders fall on their faces and worship God. They declare that God has begun to reign and proclaim that the time of judgment and the rewarding of his servants has now come. The Temple of God in heaven is then opened and the ark of the covenant could be seen. Flashes of lightning, peals of thunder, an earthquake and a severe hailstorm came from the Temple.

Following the cycle of the seven seals and the seven trumpets, John sees two great signs in heaven. One is of a gloriously cosmic woman who is pregnant, and the other is that of an enormous red dragon. Their stories will be told in chapter five.

Before the pouring out of the seven bowls, John sees what looks like a sea of glass glowing with fire. Those who had been victorious over the beast stand beside the sea. They are each given harps by God and sing the song of Moses and the Lamb. John then sees the Temple in heaven. Seven angels dressed in white with golden sashes around their necks come out of the Temple with seven plagues. One of the four living creatures gives a golden bowl filled with the wrath of God to each of the seven angels. The temple is then filled with the smoke of the presence of God's glory and nobody can enter the Temple until the seven plagues of the seven angels is complete. With the pouring out of the seven bowls, the wrath of God will be complete.

When the first angel pours out his bowl, sores and boils break out on all who have the mark of the beast and worship his image. The second bowl is poured out on the sea. The waters turn to blood and every creature in the sea dies. The third angel pours out a bowl on all rivers and springs of waters and they too are turned to blood. The fourth bowl is poured out on the sun and the heat of the sun scorches people with fire. The people curse God but refuse to repent. The fifth angel pours his bowl on the throne of the beast and the entire kingdom was plunged into darkness. People gnawed their tongues in agony but still refused to repent. The sixth angel pours out his bowl on the Euphrates River and the river dries up to prepare the way for the kings of the East.

John then sees three impure spirits that look like frogs come out of the mouths of the dragon, the beast, and the false prophet. These demonic spirits perform signs and go out to the kings of the entire world and gather them at Armageddon for the battle on the great day of God Almighty. The seventh angel pours his bowl in the air and out of the Temple a loud voice from the throne declares, "It is done." Along with flashes of lightning, peals of thunder, and rumblings, the greatest earthquake since the creation of mankind takes place. The great city splits into three parts and the cities of the nations collapse. God gives to Babylon the Great a cup filled with the wine of his wrath. Islands flee and mountains cannot be found. Huge hailstones of about a hundred pounds apiece fall onto people from the sky. The people continue to curse God because the plague is so terrible.

Historical Stage

It is abundantly clear from the opening of these six seals by the Lamb that the judgment of the Lamb is unleashed across the earth. The very Lamb who was judged and slain and appeared at the throne of God and worshipped by living creatures, elders, and angels, is now the Lamb that breaks the scrolls from which judgment rains down on the earth and its inhabitants. The beauty of worship and harmony which brought together every heavenly creature in a united voice of praise for the Lamb in heaven is in stark contrast to the chaos, destruction, ruin, and death that unfolds on the earth.

The four horses and riders are traditionally referred to as the four horsemen of the apocalypse. As each horse and rider are unveiled, a certain kind of judgment is unleashed on the earth. The various judgments encompass such things as hostility among the nations of the world, economic and social injustice, and death itself. Although the horses and their respective riders are images designed to be etched in our imagination, the impact of their activity is quite real. There aren't literally four horses with their riders racing back and forth through our world, but there are literal wars, injustices, hardships, and death.

The normal inclination is to read the judgements of the seven trumpets to be that which happens after the opening of the seven seals. This particular approach simply treats the events as if they were revealed in chronological and linear order. However, apocalyptic literature is not concerned with timelines in the same way that the orderly recording of events would be. Narratives and stories happen over time. The very fact that they take place over a period of time is what defines them as narratives and stories.

Apocalyptic images do not play by the same rules and are not bound by the same kinds of parameters associated with narratives and stories. Stepping into the apocalyptic world requires us to remove our normal lens of expecting things to unfold in chronological order. Laying aside our normal lens through which we view and experience everyday life requires intentional effort. It is only on rare occasions that we would even think of laying aside our historical lens. They are a vital part of how we live life and engage in human activity in the world. Our historical lens is as vital to living life as our eyesight would be to walking across the room or driving down the interstate.

One of the biggest missteps that is made in reading Revelation is reading it through our historical lens. When we do so, we end up trying to make apocalyptic images fit into our historical frames of reference. However, apocalyptic images cannot be tamed and neatly packaged within the contours of historical parameters. The whole point of apocalyptic literature is to take us beyond our normal confines. This is the place where we lay down our powers of reason and logic and allow our imaginations to guide us to places, peoples, and realities that cannot even be conceived otherwise.

Rather than seeing the judgments of the trumpets as subsequent to the judgments of the seals as we would in a chronological narrative, the judgments of the trumpets should be seen as concurrent with the judgments of the seals. The trumpets do not point to judgments that happen after the judgments of the seals – they point to a different perspective of the very same judgments that are unleashed with the opening of the seals. The purpose of the judgments of the seals and trumpets is not to put events on a timeline, but to enable us to see the nature of realities that we cannot see with the naked eye and that we cannot place on a timeline.

Although the events associated with apocalyptic images cannot be neatly fit into our timelines, they do depict realities that impact and shape what takes place in real time. The judgments of the seals are judgments that actually take place in the time span between the two advents of Jesus. The seals serve as a declaration that the judgment of God is a present and ongoing reality. God does respond to evil in the world and does not simply look the other way. The judgments of the trumpets speak to the same time period as those of the seals. Whereas the seals declare the reality that God judges evil, the trumpets reveal that there is an aspect of God's judgment in which judgment is partial and is intended to offer opportunities for humankind to repent.

In the cases of both the seals and the trumpets, it is clear that judgment falls on both creation and humankind. The first four seal judgments and the first four trumpet judgments focus on creation. The fifth and sixth seal and trumpet judgments focus on humanity. The partial and redemptive nature of the judgments associated with the trumpets are seen in the repeated use of one third throughout the entire trumpet judgments. The judgment is real, but it is also partial. Just as the seals depict in apocalyptic imagery the *reality* of judgment that takes place between the first and second coming of Christ, the trumpets depict in apocalyptic imagery the *partial nature* and *redemptive purpose* of the judgment during the two comings of Christ.

There are several features of the bowl plagues that cannot go unnoticed. When compared to the judgments associated with the opening of the seals and the blowing of the trumpets, the judgments of the bowls are more intense and encompass the entirety of creation and humankind. No longer is there partial destruction and partial loss of life – the impact now is total. Whereas, the seals speak to the *reality* of judgment and the trumpets speak to the *partial* nature of judgment, the bowls speak to the ultimate *finality* of judgment.

The finality of judgment is also seen in the fact that with the pouring out of the bowls of wrath there is no interlude as there was between the sixth and seventh seals and the sixth and seventh trumpets. There are no images of God's protection, no stopping of the action to reassure the faithful that God has sealed them or has gathered them as his own. The purpose of the bowl judgments is to point clearly and forcefully to the reality that there is a finality of God's judgments. Although his judgments are intended to bring about repentance and to restore relationship with humankind, those who curse God are only hardened and refuse to repent.

It would be impossible for Hebrew and Christian readers to not see the obvious connections between the judgments of the bowls and the relationship to the story of Israel's redemption from Egypt. The opening scene of a fiery red glass sea points back to such images as the plague on the Nile River turning to blood and to the Red Sea where the Hebrew children escaped to the desert by crossing on dry land. Those who had been victorious over the beast stand safely beside the sea and sing the song of Moses and the Lamb. The various plagues such as boils, bodies of water turned to blood, darkness, frogs, and death itself, are all images rooted and embedded in the story of Israel. Although the apocalyptic images of the judgment of the seals, trumpets, and bowls are horrific and terrifying, the judgments are cast in the far greater scheme of God's redemptive activity. The judgments themselves cry out for salvation and seek to do everything possible to bring about the repentance of mankind.

Contemporary Reflection

There are a number of reasons as to why many people do not wish to read the book of Revelation and there are likewise a number of reasons why many who do read the book of Revelation do not know *how* to read it. As we have pointed out, Revelation is written in an apocalyptic literary style which aims for the imagination. When these two critical pieces are set aside, what emerges out of the pages of this sacred text are often more bewildering than the images that are in the text!

Perhaps the most troubling of all matters for most readers of Revelation has to do with the prolific and horrific images of judgment. No one could possibly deny that with the opening of the seals, the blowing of the trumpets, and the pouring out of the bowls that the ensuing judgments may have seemed to be beyond imagination itself. The graphic intensity is overwhelming and if we are not attuned to the nature of apocalyptic language as speaking to our imagination, we will drown in a dark sea of confusion, despair, and hopelessness.

Whether we ignore or become obsessed with images of judgment, the reality is that the judgment of God can be an intimidating and challenging topic of conversation for any of us. Among the contributing factors as to why this is a particularly challenging topic are these realities: we are fearful of judgment, we have a limited view of judgment, and we have a negative view of judgment. The book of Revelation – along with the entire scope of Scripture – offers a perspective on God's judgment that challenges our basic presuppositions and our common misconceptions regarding judgment. Since the judgment scenes come to a climax and culmination in Revelation, let's explore what they have to say to us.

Judgment is a present reality.

One of the most common mistakes that is made in interpreting Revelation is interpreting the events as future events only. Without an understanding of the nature of apocalyptic literature it is easy to see why this misstep takes place. The images of judgment associated with the seals, trumpets, and bowls are nowhere to be seen in our current historical context. We may see images on our newsfeeds of such things as destruction, oppression, lawlessness, homelessness, and much more, but we don't see such things as apocalyptic horsemen, the raining down of a hundred-pound hailstones, the darkening of the sun, the sea turning to blood, or demonic spirits in the form of frogs.

Since we do not see the images of Revelation in our particular historical situation, it is tempting to cast the images off to the side and regard them as irrelevant or to cast them into the future and regard them as descriptions of what has not yet been realized. Both options miss the point entirely. Revelation is a revealing of what God is doing now. The graphic and detailed images are simply ways for us to see what we could not otherwise see. The images give us sight into realities that are happening right now which we cannot see. Yet, we live in the daily matrix of these unseen realities. Just because we do not see them does not mean they are not real.

The judgments associated with the seals, trumpets, and bowls are both highly relevant and already present. This ties in directly with the two-advent eschatology in which we are living in between the first and second comings of Christ. With the first coming of Jesus, the Kingdom was inaugurated and through his ministry was already present. We are not waiting for the Kingdom to come – it has already arrived. We are waiting for the Kingdom to be consummated at the second coming of Jesus. In the same way that the Kingdom has already broken through into human history, so has God's judgment already arrived. We do not have to wait for the Kingdom to be consummated to see or experience God's judgment – judgment is here!

God's judgment is rooted in love.

Just as we may not typically think about God's judgment as a present reality, we also do not typically think about judgment from a biblical perspective of judgment nor an adequate grasp of God's nature of love. Our view of judgment is deeply rooted in the notion that it emerges as a violent act of vengeance on its subjects. Consequently, we tend to view the judgment of God as an act of vengeance directed at us because of our sin and brokenness.

Throughout the entire witness of Scripture God is depicted as a God of love, compassion, mercy, and grace. God's very nature and character is that of love. God's judgment is not an act in which his love is suspended so that his wrath can be unleashed. Rather, his love is what drives his judgment. God does not put his love aside in order to exercise judgment.

The notion that God is love even in his acts of judgment and wrath is a very challenging reality to get our minds and hearts around. Our inability to comprehend that God's judgments flow from his love creates a tension in us that does not exist for God. Even very competent readers of Scripture have struggled with the notion of the relationship between God's love and God's wrath. This has led many readers of Scripture to frame the tension in terms of the difference between the Old Testament God and the New Testament God. It is claimed by some that the God depicted in the Old Testament is vengeful and wrathful whereas the God depicted in the New Testament is loving and compassionate. This unhealthy and heretical concept is simply a reflection of how deeply challenging it is to grasp that God's judgments do in fact flow from his love.

God's love and God's wrath are not even two sides of the same coin. It is not the case that God's judgment is the absence of his love. God's very nature is love – it always has been and always will be. This is not to suggest that God's love is a soft kind of love that does not respond to evil and wrong. To the contrary, God's love is such a strong and infinite love that it is thoroughly compelled to respond to evil and wrong in terms of judgment. This is not the kind of love and grace that does not care what we do, but the kind that cares more about us than we do for our own selves.

The depth of the images of his judgment with seals, trumpets, and bowls is only a reflection of the depth of his love for all of creation and every creature within it. His love is so deep that at great cost to himself he gave his only Son so that there could be a grand and complete restoration of all things unto himself.

God's judgment is an invitation to us to share in the process of restoration.

The restoring of all things to newness is a deep and lengthy process. It is in fact the process which stretches the entire scope of the Bible from Genesis to Revelation. The entire activity of God in the biblical drama is obsessed and consumed with the process of reconciliation and restoration. There is not a single page of Scripture in which this is not the overarching story and the underlying current.

It is the very nature of love itself to share it with others. Love that is not shared is not love at all. It would have been a much easier fix for God to have simply declared for all things to be made new. It is not that God couldn't do such a thing – it is that God didn't do such a thing. His love for the world with all of its broken and messy fractures is so great that he could not refrain from inviting the very ones who are responsible for our human condition to partner with him in restoring the entire project. It is this very process which makes the story of God and of his redemptive mission in the world the most significant story in the entire universe.

It is because of his love that God chose the old man Abraham to be the father of a nation and chose the oppressed Israelites to be the instrument of salvation to the entire world. It was in love that he chose his sinless Son to be the sacrifice which bore our sin and guilt. It was because of love that he chose Paul as the suffering apostles to the Gentiles. The story of reconciliation is a story of God's love for humanity and his presence in humanity to bring about reconciliation.

God's judgments are divine offers to us to join him in the great restoration adventure. Judgment gives us the opportunity to say *no* to the building of our own personal projects whatever they may be and to say *yes* to the redemptive mission of God in and for the world. It is through his present acts and engagements of judgment that we often find that turning away from selfish pursuits and turning toward God's redemptive pursuit brings forgiveness, wholeness, meaning, and fruitfulness. This is what repentance is all about. We are trading whatever story we are living in to live in God's story.

The joy of love is that even if we fall into it, it takes a lifetime to live in it. We may experience love in an unexpected instant, the working out of love is a process that extends into all of time and eternity. Although God is fully capable of using divine fiat to accomplish his purposes of full reconciliation, he chose the long-term process of love working out through relationships. One of his greatest tools in bringing humanity to the greatest story that could ever be experienced is his love-shaped judgment.

Judgment is indicative of the freedom that God has given us.

As human beings, we are made in the image of God. Although we all share in a common humanity, our humanity is revealed through us in such ways that every single one of us is uniquely distinct. The same thing is true of being made in the image of God – although we are all made in the image of God, the image is displayed through us in a host of various ways so that it does not look exactly the same way in any two people.

An essential part of being human and being made in the image of God is that we are bestowed with the gift of freedom. We are free to choose how we wish to live out our humanity and we are free as to how we wish to be bearers of the image of God. It is this freedom that allows us to choose paths of love, service, humility, and goodness or paths of hatred, selfishness, pride, and ruin. God's choice to grant us this kind of freedom comes with vulnerabilities and danger. We are all vulnerable to the lure of sin and destruction and we all fall for it. We are all infected by sin and we all die.

Sin and death are a high price to pay for the freedom which we have all been granted. Yet, without this kind of freedom we could not be genuinely human, and we could not live in genuinely human relationships among ourselves or with God. When freedom is co-opted by sin, every imaginable relationship goes sideways – including our relationship with both creation and the Creator.

The judgment of God signifies God's response to the destructive nature of sin and the ruinous impact it has in every dimension of life. As we have pointed out above, God's judgments are rooted in his love. God has not separated himself from us, we have separated ourselves from God. Judgment is the primary means by which God invites us back to the kind of freedom in which we are truly made free – the freedom to love God, to love people, and to love creation. Any other promise of freedom is a pseudo freedom which only promises to captivate, oppress, and destroy what it is to be genuinely free human beings who genuinely reflect the image of God in our world.

Judgment brings about justice.

As a means for setting things right again, God's judgment brings about justice. As a God who is defined by love, God seeks justice. The book of Revelation is filled with both undertones and overtones to such grand stories as the Exodus and to such messengers as the prophets. The entire story of the Exodus is in reality a justice story. God's people had been oppressed by the Egyptians for over 400 years. The call of Moses was a call to go down to Egypt and rescue the children of Abraham. The promises that had been made to Abraham generations ago were being held captive by the Egyptians.

The deliverance of the Hebrews from captivity is the greatest act of liberation and justice in the entire story of the Hebrews as a nation. The unfulfilled promises made to Abraham finally begin to take shape and become a living reality. The nation would have its own land, its own kingdom, and eventually produce a messiah. In so doing, the entire world would be blessed and through the weakness and brokenness of Israel's own story, the hope of restoration through Jesus the Messiah would be offered to all peoples, nations, tribes, and languages.

The cry and admonition for justice is loudly heard through the voice of the prophets. The prophets are not predictors of future events but proclaimers of God's justice in the world. Their voices and actions are deeply embedded with the call for justice to be restored. Just as in our own current historical contexts, the call for justice was often on behalf of those who were abused, oppressed, poor, and marginalized. It was a call often against the powerful political and even religious leaders who were the ones through whose hands such abuses were often felt..

Whether the thunderous voices of the prophets were aimed at the powerful and wealthy, or the people on the street and in the market squares, the intent never wavered. God's words through the prophets are intended to make things right again. As such, these words often came in the form of prophetic judgments against any who stood in the way of God's working to make things right. The cries of the prophets for justice were often met with resistance and ended up in death for the ones who dared proclaim the message. Yet, the voice of the prophets thunder forth still through the pages of Revelation and into our world today.

Judgment is necessary for the establishing of God's Kingdom on the earth.

The Kingdom of God refers most simply and broadly to the rule and reign of God. The biblical story is one that could be told in terms of creation, fall, redemption, and new creation. This is the story line which extends from Genesis to Revelation. The Kingdom of God is actually established on the earth. The full transformation and reconciliation of creation and humanity back to God is the vision of the Kingdom of God.

As we have been pointing out through this entire conversation, God's judgment is primarily the means through which that which is wrong is made right, that which is broken is made whole. It is in this sense that we long for judgment to take place and cry out for its swift arrival and its full consummation. Once God's judgment has sorted all things out and everything in the Kingdom is just as it should be, the new creation becomes our new and eternal reality. The intense judgment scenes in Revelation are absolutely essential to the hope of the new creation.

The real issue when it comes to the judgment of God is whether or not we trust the God who does the judging. Do we trust the Lamb who bears the mark of being slaughtered and yet lives? Judgment has a mystery about it that is well beyond our capacity to fully understand and is even further beyond our ability to administer. Perhaps this serves as a soft reminder that humans were not designed to be the mediators of judgment. Our minds cannot comprehend, our hearts are bent with selfishness, and our hands are not steady.

The root meaning of judgement in the Bible has to do with restoring that which has been lost. God's judging of the world is not rooted in a desire to crush the world that he created and loves, but to bring wholeness to a world which is shattered and light to a world which is living in darkness. The basic idea of judgment in the Bible is not about punishing evil and rewarding good. It is about reclaiming an entire creation that has felt the force of human sin and bringing and restoring the very humanity which severed the relationship.

As a means of restoration and wholeness, God's judgments are in fact, acts of mercy, grace, and compassion. Without them, all would be ruined and lost. There should be no surprise that judgment and salvation go hand in hand whether in the words of prophets or the images of Revelation. This is not to suggest that judgment does not have a severance side to it – as we shall see in what lies ahead. In all matters of judgment, we can only cling to the reality that the One who does the judging is trustworthy, faithful, and true.

Wrap Up

The book of Revelation is replete with horrific and vivid scenes of God's judgment on both creation and humanity. The primary ways in which God's judgment is depicted is through the breaking of seven seals, the blowing of seven trumpets, and the pouring out of seven bowls. These three major cycles of seven judgments are not linear or chronological. Although in the text the seven seals are followed by the seven trumpets which are then followed by the seven bowls, these three cycles refer to the same period of time – the time between the first and second coming of Christ.

For many readers of Revelation, the scenes of judgment are unbearable and difficult to square with God's love. Much of this stems from an inadequate view and incomplete understanding of God's love. God loves the world that he created so deeply and the people in the world so fervently, that he goes to every expense to bring about wholeness, renewal, and transformation. His desire runs so deep in this regard that he does not withhold his only Son. The death and resurrection of Jesus are the means through which all things are made new and reconciled to God.

When judgment is seen as flowing from the very love of God, it has the power to transform the way we read Revelation and experience the hope and salvation that it offers. Although our inclinations may be to seek refuge from the apocalyptic images of judgment in Revelation, we can in fact embrace the images once we see the heart of the God who judges and the eternal purpose of salvation to which judgment seeks to call us.

ReImagine

The seals, trumpets, and bowls represent some of the most intense and dramatic images of judgment that are found anywhere in Scripture. Many readers of Revelation struggle to see these judgments as coming from a God who is love. Reflect on how judgment is in fact an expression of God's love. In what ways does this reality help you reimagine how you read Revelation?

Just as an understanding of the function of apocalyptic literature is critical to reading Revelation, so is it critical to have an understanding of two-advent eschatology. The vast majority of Revelation actually takes place in our current historical context as living in between the two advents of Jesus. Consider how the notion of two-advent eschatology informs your reading of Revelation.

We have argued that the judgments of the seals, trumpets, and bowls are concurrent rather than consecutive. Each of them speak to a different aspect of judgment. Consider how the various visions of judgment that are represented by the seals, trumpets, and bowls help us to have a greater and fuller understanding of the nature and purpose of God's judgment in the world.

God's judgment is ultimately a measure to make things right. In what ways do you see the judgment theme of Revelation in terms of social justice? How is this different than a vision of judgment which depicts God as being vengeful and angry?

Fourth Image:
The Saving Lamb

Imagination is the voice of daring.
If there is anything godlike about God, it is that.
He dared to imagine everything.
    Henry Miller

Throughout the entire dramatic visions of the seals, trumpets and bowls, there is unquestionably the unleashing of horrific judgments of God on both creation and mankind. However, there are also images and visions of the beauty and power of God's salvation. This salvation comes in the form of God's protection of his people. This is not the kind of protection in which the people of God are saved *from* suffering and death, but the kind of protection in which God's people experience salvation *through* seasons of suffering and when they walk in the valley of death. Although suffering and death are realities for followers of the Lamb, they do not have the power to thwart the purposes and plans of God for his creation and for his people.

   As we have seen, the twin themes of judgment and salvation are especially reminiscent of the message of the prophets. The focus of the prophets is not to predict the future, but to reveal the reality of God's present judgment on such things as corrupt political power and abusive religious authority. In the same vein, Revelation is not a predictive book.

It does not seek to predict world events or to provide chronological timelines. It is exactly what it says it is – a revelation *of* Jesus Christ. It is the behind the scenes unveiling of what God is doing right now to respond to evil and to bring about the renewal of all things. His response to evil comes in the form of judgment and his work to renew all things comes in the form of salvation.

It is in this way that judgment and salvation complement each other. It is also in this way that they take place simultaneously. Although the salvation and protection images are located after the sixth seal and sixth trumpet respectively, it must be kept in mind that apocalyptic language is not seeking to place things in chronological order. The judging and the saving take place at the same time. It is not as if the judgments of God are unfolding and then are suddenly held back for a season while God then focuses his attention on the protecting and saving of his people.

Although the protecting and saving scenes are strategically placed after the sixth seal and trumpet, they are not actually interludes in real time. They are only interludes in the sense that we get to see scenes of judgment and scenes of salvation side by side as they unfold together. It is as if we see the judgment of God with one eye and the salvation of God with the other. They are happening at the very same time, and they are happening right now. The whole point of Revelation is to let us see beyond our natural vision what Jesus is doing in his work of making all things new. This work involves judging and saving and we are living right in the middle of it all.

Behind the Scenes

John sees four angels standing at the four corners of the earth. The angels hold back the winds that blow across the land and seas. John then sees another angel coming from the east having the seal of the living God. With a loud voice the angel from the east calls out to the four angels at the corners of the earth to not harm the land or the sea until the seal of the living God has been placed on the foreheads of the servants of God.

The number of those sealed is 144,000 – a number that represents 12,000 from each of the 12 tribes of Israel. John then sees a great multitude of people standing before the throne of God. The multitude consists of people of every nation, tribe, people and language. The vast number of those in the multitude could not even be counted. They stand in front of the Lamb wearing white robes and holding palm branches in their hands and cry out with a loud voice, "Salvation belongs to our God, who sits on the throne and to the Lamb." All the angels fall down on their faces before the throne and render a chorus of Amens.

One of the elders then reveals to John that those in white robes are the ones that have come out of the great tribulation and whose robes have been washed and made white by the blood of the Lamb. They are ever before the throne of God by night and by day and would no longer face hunger, thirst, and scorching sun. The Lamb at the center of the throne will be their shepherd and lead them to springs of living water.

John sees a mighty angel coming down from heaven. The angel is robed in a cloud, has a rainbow above his head, his face is shining like the sun, and his legs are like pillars of fire. In his hand is a small open scroll. With his right foot planted on the sea and his left foot planted on the land, he gives a loud shout like the roar of a lion. John was about to write what he heard but was commanded by the voices of the seven thunders not to write anything down.

Raising his right hand to heaven, the angel swears by him who lives forever that there would be no more delay. John is then instructed by a voice from heaven to take the scroll from the hand of the angel. When John asks the angel for the scroll, the angel tells him to take and eat it. The scroll tastes like honey in his mouth but turns sour in his stomach. John is then told that he must prophesy about many peoples, languages, nations, and kings.

John is then commanded to measure the Temple of God and the altar but to not measure the outer court of the Gentiles. The Gentiles would trample the holy city for 42 months. God would appoint two witnesses dressed in sackcloth to prophesy for 1,260 days. The two witnesses are two olive trees and two lampstands that stand before the

Lord. *Fire comes out of their mouth to anyone who tries to harm them. They have power to keep the rain from coming down from the heavens, of turning water into blood, and striking the earth with any kind of plague at will.*

When the witnesses finish their prophesying, the beast from the Abyss attacks and kills them. Their bodies lie in the open square for three and a half days and are refused burial. People gloat over them and celebrate their deaths by the sending of gifts to each other. After three and half days the breath of life enters them, and they stand to their feet. All those who see them are terrified. The two witnesses are then taken up to heaven in a cloud. At that very hour there is a severe earthquake and a tenth of the city collapses. Seven thousand people are killed. The rest are terrified and give glory to God.

Historical Stage

The two separate groups of people that John sees in the interlude between the sixth and seventh seals are in fact the same group of people – they are all God's people. It cannot be reiterated enough that apocalyptic language is intentionally nonliteral. The number 144,000 does not represent a head count of the number of people that John saw. Rather, it represents a totality or completion of the people of God. This reality comes to expression in the second vision where John sees an innumerable number of people.

Just as the counter images of Lion and Lamb enable us to see a much more fully developed picture of Jesus, the images of 144,000 from the tribes of Israel and the innumerably vast crowd before the throne enables us to see a much more fully developed picture of God's people. It is a way of suggesting that although the number of those saved is innumerable, God knows every one of them. The power of apocalyptic language is that it enables us to get beyond the logic of things and invites us into the sheer mystery of the ways of God.

The purpose of these two visions is to reveal that amidst the judgments that are being rained down on both creation and humanity, God seals and protects his people. This does not mean that they are saved *from* the great tribulation but are saved *through* the great tribulation. In his salutation to the readers, John states that he is a fellow companion in their suffering. Yet, through his suffering and exile to the island of Patmos, John is spared to be the one to whom and through whom the great revelation of God is revealed. It is not the case that the followers of Jesus will not suffer, but that their suffering will not lead to banishment from God – even if it does lead to their deaths and martyrdoms. Neither should it be lost on us that the very one who opens the seals from which judgment and suffering ensue is himself a suffering Lamb.

God's protection and salvation in both the vision of the 144,000 and the vision of the vast number of people are depicted in very different ways. In the case of the 144,000, a seal is placed on their foreheads. The image of a seal flows directly from the seals that were on the scroll of God which only the Lamb could open. Just as the seals on the scroll identify the scroll as specifically belonging to God, the seals on the foreheads of the 144,000 identify the people as specifically belonging to God. Both the scroll and the people are God's and only the slain Lamb can break the seals on the scroll and also make it possible for the 144,000 to receive the seal of God on their foreheads.

In the second scene where John sees a great multitude from every nation, tribe, people and language, God's protection and salvation is evidenced by the fact that they are all wearing white robes and holding palm branches and are all standing before the throne and before the Lamb. The white robes are indicative of righteousness, purity, and victory. Palm branches were commonly used to celebrate the entrance of an army returning home after a victorious battle with their treasures and trophies.

In a very nuanced and almost unnoticed way, the Lamb who is before the throne of God is also the shepherd of those who are donned in white and stand before the throne. The image of a lamb as also being a shepherd does not make logical sense. In the world of apocalyptic language and imagery this is not a problem at all. In fact, the very tension between the images serves to magnify the greater tension between the reality of judgment and the reality of salvation as they meet together in the very same world of lived experience.

The interlude between the sixth and seventh trumpets functions in the same way as the interlude between the sixth and seventh seals. The judgments on both creation and humanity have been intense. But now there is a momentary measure of hope and protection. The mighty angel which comes down from heaven has features that are reminiscent of the opening vision of Christ which John sees. Unlike the case of the scroll in which the Lamb breaks the seals and judgments are unleashed, the scroll in the angel's hand is open and John is commanded to eat it.

The fact that the contents of the smaller scroll are not revealed suggests that there are some parts of the story of God which are known only to God and remain a mystery to humanity. Eating the scroll is a dramatic act which signifies that John is to ingest the contents of the scroll. While the contents taste sweet in his mouth, they turn sour in his stomach. This represents the very nature of the prophetic word that brings both salvation and judgment. The taste of salvation is sweet in the mouth, but the effect of judgment is sour in the stomach. There is not a sweet scroll and a sour scroll – simply a scroll with one message that has a dual effect.

The measuring of the Temple and the altar points to the reality of God's measure of protection surrounding his people. Although the inner courts experience the salvation of God, the outer courts experience the judgment of God. The Gentiles trample on God's city for 42 months and the two witnesses prophesy for 1,260 days. The two numbers represent the same length of time – three and a half years. Here we see that numbers in apocalyptic literature carry specific meanings. Although the time period is exactly the same, the forty-two months is associated with a period of evil and the 1,260 days is associated with a period of good.

The two witnesses recall the ministries of Elijah and Moses. Elijah is the prophet that contested the 450 prophets of Baal at Mount Carmel in which God sent a fireball from heaven to consume his offering. He is also the prophet who prayed that the rain would be held back from the land for three and a half years. Moses is the prophet that God sent to Pharoah to bring the captive Israelites out of Egypt and through whom God wrought judgments in the form of plagues. Like the two witnesses of Revelation, both Moses and Elijah share traditions that God took them to heaven in a cloud.

The two witnesses are clothed in sackcloth which serves as a vivid image of repentance. As we have seen previously, the judgments of God are intended to offer the opportunity for repentance for those who hear the message. Many, however, reject the invitation to repentance and eventually experience the full weight of God's judgment. When the two prophets complete their words and work of bearing testimony, a beast emerging from the Abyss attacks, overpowers, and kills the witnesses.

For three and a half days the bodies of the two witnesses lay exposed in the public square. People from every tribe, nation, and language gaze upon their corpses but refuse them burial. The inhabitants of the earth gloat over them and celebrate by sending gifts to each other. After the three and a half days, the breath of God enters them, and they stand to their feet. Those who see them are struck with terror. A loud voice from heaven calls to them and they ascend to heaven in a cloud as their enemies look on. At that very hour an intense earthquake collapses a tenth of the city and seven thousand people are killed. The survivors are terrified and give glory to God.

The two witnesses, also referred to as the two olive trees and the two lampstands, are symbolic of the anointing presence of God's Spirit. The fates of the two witnesses bear significant resemblance to that of Jesus himself. After three days they are raised and whisked up to heaven in a cloud. Although the ministry of the two witnesses leads to their respective deaths at the hands of the beast, both are revived by God's breath and are taken to heaven. The judgment that falls upon the city is partial and in this case the repentance of those who lived seems to be widespread. The judgment of God has accomplished its purpose of bringing about salvation.

Contemporary Reflection

It would be easy to be so overwhelmed by the images of judgment associated with the seven seals, seven trumpets, and seven bowls, that the images of salvation fall between the cracks. The obsession that many readers have with the scenes of judgment can sometimes leave little oxygen in the room for taking a breath of salvation. However, it would be an act of gross misreading of Revelation to gloss over the images which speak directly to what God is doing with his people as his judgments unfold across the earth. Here are some insights about salvation that will help guide our engagement of Revelation.

Salvation is rooted in the love of God.

Although it may have come somewhat as a challenging notion that God's judgment is rooted in his love, there is no shock whatsoever to the notion that salvation is rooted in the love of God. The very need for salvation is a confession that both humanity and creation are profoundly broken. Even when each of them are at their most glorious moment of beauty or achievement, neither of them can save themselves. The depth of brokenness extends much deeper and broader than any promise of salvation apart from God could ever offer.

It is only because God is love that the possibility of salvation even exists. It is not that there is a part of God that is love, but that the very nature and being of God is love. Everything – even his judgment – flows from the essence and nature of his perfect and everlasting love. Every other attribute of God flows from his love. This simple oversight is often missed when we talk about God's character and attributes. There is a vast difference between love as one of the many attributes of God and love as the very essence of God from which all other attributes flow.

When understood in this context, salvation is not just one of the many projects that God has going on in the world – it is *the* project. Everything flows into the vast ocean of salvation or flows from it. God has put his entire being and energy into this one project of salvation. God's Kingdom is not one of oppression and tyranny, but one of salvation. He does not reign with a hammer in his hand, but with a cross in his heart.

As we have pointed out earlier, the so-called interludes of salvation in Revelation are not interludes where God steps out of his wrath and judgment to offer protection to his people before returning once again to his acts of judgment. The interludes are only interludes in the story line of Revelation. The images of salvation reflect all of God's work of salvation throughout all history – not just his work of salvation before the final seals and trumpets. Lest the judgments cloud our vision of God's love, the salvation scenes serve as ever reminders that in all things God is love.

Salvation is an ongoing process.

A great deal of our understanding and language of salvation in evangelical circles usually focuses on salvation as a singular event in a person's life. For many people, the initial experience of salvation is dramatic, and the details can be recalled with vividness including the exact circumstances, day, and time in which it was experienced. For others, the experience of initial salvation is less dramatic, and the details not easily recalled or known.

Regardless of the varied and unique stories and testimonies surrounding the experience of salvation, it is an ongoing process for all who enter into it. Salvation is not just the crossing of a threshold – it is the entire journey which ensues. Even though it may be a little mind blowing, the work of salvation was even taking place before we embraced it as a gift in our life. It may be something like stepping outside of our house into a beautiful sunny day. We feel the warmth of the sun's rays on our body and bask in the joy which it brings. Our initial experience, however, does not mean that the sun started shining at that very moment. The sun does what the sun does every single moment of the day and night, we just happened to experience it in a certain way on a certain day. Even before we step outside, the sun is already chasing away the last vestiges of night and seeking to flood into our homes through every window and door that it possibly can. It is simply waiting for us to step into its warmth and light.

Once we cross the threshold into the sunlight, the sun does not stop shining. In fact, it does not even stop shining when evening comes. Salvation works in a very similar way. It is an ongoing reality in our lives regardless of the time of day or the season of our life. The ongoing process of salvation is unceasing and unwavering. The experience of salvation is not a one-time commitment to the Lamb, but an ongoing and unending relationship with him.

God's protection and salvation of his people in the scenes between the sixth and seventh seals and the sixth and seventh trumpets, are depicted as ongoing salvation realities. The break in the story line is not intended to suggest that there is a momentary experience of salvation. Rather, it is a depiction of an unfolding reality of salvation that we experience as an ongoing process. Even before creation itself, God was mysteriously engaged in the very salvation which his people would experience.

Salvation is both personal and corporate.

For many evangelicals, salvation is individual and refers to the saving of the soul. The salvation scenes in Revelation paint a much larger picture than many of our traditional visions of salvation. There is undoubtedly the notion of individual salvation in the Bible. However, the scope of salvation is much broader than the saving of individual souls.

It is clear that the salvation images depict salvation not so much as a loose collection of saved individuals but as a gathering of people who are bound together as one humanity. Whether described in terms of 144,000 people, those gathered around the throne from every tribe and nation, the measuring of the God's people in the Temple, and even the two witnesses who were killed and raised from the dead, salvation is depicted as something larger than an individual experience.

We are not saved to be alone; we are saved to form a new community. This is why terms such as family, brother, and sister, have such deep impact and meaning. These biblical ways of referring to each other depict how salvation redefines the nature of our relationships with each other. People from every generation and from all parts of the world are intimately connected together through the sacrifice of the Lamb. It is not as if we all live in the same zip code but that we all live in the same household.

The beautiful and powerful vision of salvation portrayed in the Revelation scenes speaks directly and forcefully to the reality that the family of God is one family. It is not to be divided by denominations, styles of worship, or even theological differences. The people of God are defined totally and fully by the Lamb. Blessed be the day when everything that gets in the way of God's people living in unity as one people are forever gone, and we can celebrate without hindrance the reality that we are one people.

Salvation is the alignment of people and creation with God's Kingdom.

Sin is the greatest disrupter of all time. It has single handedly thrown the entire order of humanity and creation into chaos. No one has escaped the reach of sin. Even the sinless Lamb of God bears eternally the marks of sin on his own body. The power of sin is that it separates every single one of us from God. The separation is so deep and disturbing that it can only be referred to in terms of death – a complete severance from life.

With the inbreaking of God's Kingdom through the presence and ministry of Jesus the very powers of sin and death are put on final notice. Every single word and deed of Jesus is directly related to the revealing of God's Kingdom. Although the Kingdom will be consummated in the blink of an eye at the return of Jesus, it is being worked out every single day from his first advent to his second advent. The total disruption and misalignment of humanity and creation is even now in the process of being aligned with God's Kingdom.

The salvation scenes in Revelation depict the people of God as a people who are fully aligned with God's Kingdom. They have been sealed, robed, and measured. They only wait for the finale in which the Kingdom is fully established on the earth. In that day of fulfillment, the Kingdom will be fully established and all of God's people and all of God's creation will be fully and forever filled and aligned with God's Kingdom.

Salvation reflects the sovereignty of God.

Although the images and language of Revelation may be confusing to many readers, it is clear throughout the entirety of Revelation that God is sovereign. He is intimately involved in world events and exercises control over how these events play out. Regardless of how the story of Revelation is interpreted, there would be little dissent as to the fact that God is depicted as expressing his will and being in control. God holds the scroll from which the story of his Kingdom unfolds. The events that flow from the breaking of the seals, the blowing of the trumpets, and the pouring out of the bowls are all under God's expressed control.

The assertion that God is sovereign is easy enough to support, however, there is a great deal of disagreement and confusion as to *how* God exerts his sovereignty. Does being in control mean that he controls everything that happens? Does God practice any measure of self-limitation when it comes to sovereignty? Does sovereignty suggest that everything is predetermined and unalterable?

One of the most current divisive issues has to do with the sovereignty of God as it relates to predestination and election. Does God predestine who goes to heaven and even those who go to hell? The debates surrounding this issue are often heated and emotional. The salvation scenes in Revelation may offer some insight. It is clear that God protects and saves his people through the judgments that are unleashed. Nowhere throughout the salvation scenes is God depicted as choosing *who* will be included as his people. He is depicted, however, as choosing *how* his people will be protected and saved through the judgments.

Any sense of predestination in the salvation scenes are relative to the fact that God has predestined none other than Jesus to be both the Lion of Judah and the slain Lamb of God. Jesus is clearly the one who has been predestined and elected to exercise a uniquely redemptive role in the cosmic story of salvation. As it relates to God's people, predestination has to do with the role that God's people play in the mission of the Kingdom right now and in the reality that ultimately God's people are predestined to be like Jesus himself.

This is precisely the kind of sovereignty that is reflected in the salvation scenes. It is a sovereignty that is about the fulfillment of the mission of God's Kingdom, not about who is elected to be a part of the Kingdom and who is not. This is the kind of sovereignty that flows from the reality of God's essence and nature of being a God of love. Sovereignty is the full expression of God's love. It is *how* God reigns in his Kingdom not *who* is determined to be in his Kingdom.

Wrap Up

Judgment and salvation can never be separated – they are intricately related. They need each other for their very existence. It is impossible to talk about one without talking about the other. The relationship between them is powerfully depicted in Revelation. Scenes of great judgment associated with the breaking of the seals and the blowing of the trumpets are interrupted with scenes of the even greater measure of God's salvation of his people.

After the breaking of the sixth seal and the judgment that flows from it, there is a break in scene as John sees two groups of people. The first group of people is specifically identified as being 144,000 members from the twelve tribes of Israel. The second group consists of an innumerable number of people from all nations, tribes, peoples, and languages. A literalistic reading of this scene would suggest that these are two different groups of people. This is to miss the point of how apocalyptic language functions.

The two groups do not refer to the fact that salvation for the Jews is different than salvation for the Gentiles. Nor is it intended to imply that there are two different peoples that make up the people of God. Rather, in apocalyptic fashion, the two groups that John sees in the vision are actually two visions of one group of people. The story of salvation has coursed its way through the long history of Israel, but it flowed right into the larger scene of the entire world. The vision is not intended to suggest that Israel and the Christian community make up two separate groups of people, but that the two groups are in fact the one and same people.

The vision of salvation following the sixth trumpet features the Temple of God and two faithful witnesses. John is given a measuring reed and is commanded to measure the Temple of God and its altar with its worshippers. The outer courts, however, are not to be measured. The image reflects the reality that God's people are safely protected, while those on the outside are not protected.

God will send his two prophets to those who belong to those on the outside of the Temple and the altar. These two witnesses represent two olive trees from which God's Spirit flows. The two witnesses will meet their fate of death and will be left in the streets of the city for three and a half days. They are refused burial as the inhabitants of the city gloat over their demise and celebrate with the giving of gifts to each other. When the breath of God's life enters them after the three and half days, they rise to their feet and return to heaven in a cloud. At that very hour there was an earthquake and destruction which collapses a portion of the city and kills a portion of the citizens. The terrified survivors gave glory to God.

Salvation is not just a major theme of Scripture, it is the consummate theme of Scripture. The entirety of the biblical narrative rests on the story of salvation and redemption. It is much easier to see how the salvation story plays out at the end of the book of Revelation when the triumph of Jesus is complete and evil is defeated. It may not be as easy to see how the salvation theme is present throughout other parts of Revelation. However, the salvation scenes after the sixth seal and the sixth trumpet are powerful images of the unfolding work of salvation that is taking place even as horrific scenes of judgment are underway. The so-called interludes of salvation are in reality not interludes at all – they are the story.

ReImagine

The images of salvation in Revelation are much broader and deeper than the images that many of us are accustomed to. Most of the prevailing images of salvation focus on having a personal relationship with God. Although this is certainly true, consider ways in which the images of salvation expand beyond personal relationship. In what ways does a more biblically and expansive vision of salvation reshape our understanding of such things as evangelism?

Images of salvation and judgment are intimately intertwined in Revelation. The relationship between them is necessary. Although both of them are rooted deeply in the love of God, they look so very different. Reflect on ways that salvation and judgment are inseparable. In what ways might this lead to how we envision such things as spiritual formation or spiritual warfare?

One of the most divisive topics among followers of Jesus is that of God's sovereignty. There is little disagreement as to the notion that God is sovereign. The controversy actually has to do with the meaning of God's sovereignty and in what ways is God sovereign. Consider how the judgment scenes and the salvation images in Revelation might help inform our thinking and conversation about the sovereignty of God.

Fifth Image:
The Infant Christ

Reality can be beaten with enough imagination.
Mark Twain

The scene of the infant Christ takes place in the very center of Revelation. The judgments of the seals and of the trumpets have passed. The judgments of the bowls are yet to come. This center piece moment in the story sets the cosmic images of a pregnant woman, a dragon, a sea beast, and a land beast in full descriptive images. In contrast to these full-blown apocalyptic depictions is the most simple and brief story of the birth of a male child and the immediate ascent to heaven after birth. The contrast between all the other characters and the male infant could not be greater.

In a book where the judgments of God and the characters of evil are on full display, this particular image of Jesus is one in which he is depicted in his infancy and is consequently in the most humble and vulnerable position imaginable. He is helpless against the dragon that stands ready to devour his life and if it were not for the fact that he is immediately taken to heaven after his birth, he would have certainly come to a swift ruin and death.

After the male child is transported to heaven, the woman becomes the next potential victim of the dragon. Along with the dragon, the sea beast and land beast form an evil of trinity which in many ways is a mockery of the holy trinity of Father, Son, and Spirit. The primary weapon of the trinity of evil is deception – the very kind of deception which goes all the way back to the Garden of Eden. Just as Adam and Eve were deceived into believing that the fruit from the Tree of the Knowledge of Good and Evil would make them to be like God, the masses of humanity are led to believe that this alliance between the dragon and the two beasts is a holy one rather than an unholy one. It is this deception that causes people to worship these monstrous entities and to fall into the hellish grasp of their mockery and lies.

Behind the Scenes

John sees a great sign in heaven – a woman clothed with the sun, with the moon under her feet, and a crown of twelve stars on her head. She is about to give birth to a child and cries out in pain. Then another sign appears in heaven – an enormous red dragon with seven heads and ten horns and seven crowns on its heads. With its tail, it sweeps a third of the stars from the sky and hurls them to the earth. As the woman is about to give birth, the dragon stands in front of her ready to devour the child that is born. When the male child is born, he is snatched up to God and his throne. The woman then flees to the wilderness where she is protected for 1,260 days.

War then breaks out in heaven between Michael and his angels and the dragon and his angels. The great dragon known variously as the serpent, the devil, and Satan, is hurled down to the earth with his angels. The dragon pursues the woman who gave birth to the male child. The woman is given two wings like that of an eagle and flies to the place in the desert prepared for her. The serpent spews water like a river from his mouth to sweep away the woman. The earth helps the woman by swallowing the river that is spewed from the mouth of the dragon. Enraged with the woman, the dragon goes off and makes war with the rest of her offspring.

As the dragon stands on the shore of the sea, John sees a beast coming out of the sea. The beast has ten horns and seven heads, with ten crowns on its horns and a blasphemous name on each of its heads. The beast resembles a leopard but has feet like a bear and a mouth like a lion.

The dragon gives to the beast his power, his throne, and great authority. One of the heads of the beast has a seemingly fatal wound which has been healed. People worship both the dragon and the beast. The beast is given power to utter blasphemies and exercise authority for forty-two months. It is also given power to wage war against God's people and to conquer them. Furthermore, it is given authority over every tribe, people, language, and nation. All the inhabitants of the earth whose names are not written in the Lamb's book of life worship the beast.

John then sees a second beast coming out of the earth. This beast has two horns like a lamb but speaks like a dragon. It exercises all the authority of the first beast and causes the people of the world to worship the first beast whose fatal head wound has been healed. It also performs great signs and causes fire to come down from heaven. It causes the people of the earth to set up an image of the beast whose head had been wounded. The land beast is also given power to give breath to the image of the sea beast so that the image could speak and kill all those who refused to worship it. The beast also forced all people to get a mark on their right hand or foreheads so that they could not buy or sell without the mark. The number of the beast is the number of humanity – 666.

Historical Stage

The sign that John sees in heaven is the most concise depiction of the story of Jesus that could possibly be imagined. It is on the level of being as compact as the assertion that Jesus was born, crucified, raised on the third day, and ascended to heaven. The sign John sees collapses the entire story of Jesus into a succinct statement. The action is fast paced in light of the imminent threat that is posed to the child even from the very moment of his birth.

John describes the woman giving birth to a son who is promptly snatched up to the very throne of God as a great sign. However, the explicit identity of the mother and the child are not revealed. It is evident that the mother is endowed with cosmic features including that of the sun, moon, and stars. These kinds of images reflect back to the cosmic image of Christ in the opening scene in Revelation, but there are no exact correlations. However, the depictions surrounding each of them appear to be drawn from the same pool of apocalyptic images.

It is also significant that the woman is pregnant. It is in fact the pregnancy which makes the story compelling. In her agony of childbirth, she delivers a male child. However, before the story of the birth of the child is told, John sees yet another great sign. Unlike the glorious mother who is pregnant, an enormous red dragon appears as a monstrous being who is bent on taking the life of the child even as it comes into the world. The dragon is depicted as having seven heads and ten horns with a crown on each of its heads. Its powerful tail sweeps a third of the stars out of the sky and flings them to the earth. Standing in front of the woman, he awaits the moment in which he can devour the child – a child destined to be a ruler of nations.

When the child is born, he is immediately snatched up to heaven and the woman flees for her life and seeks refuge in the wilderness. A war then breaks out in heaven between Michael and the dragon. In defeat, the great dragon is hurled down to the earth with his angels. The dragon is identified as the ancient serpent known as the devil or Satan. A loud voice in heaven proclaims that salvation and power, and the Kingdom of God, and the authority of the Messiah have come. They have triumphed by the blood of the Lamb and the testimony of martyred saints.

Once the dragon is hurled to the earth, he begins to pursue the woman who had given birth to the male child. The woman is given two wings like that of an eagle and flies into the wilderness where she was protected by God. The serpent spews water out of his mouth like a river to carry the woman away in the torrent. However, the earth opens its mouth and swallows the river that the dragon spews out. Filled with rage, the dragon wages war against the rest of the children of the woman.

This section is at the center of Revelation and serves as a centerpiece for the entire story line of Revelation. Some of the most fanciful images of characters are found in this very compact and highly apocalyptic part of the story line. The fanciful description of characters in this section has led to a number of equally fanciful interpretations. The varied fanciful interpretations of Revelation typically emerge because of a lack of understanding of the use and meaning of apocalyptic language.

The fascinating characters include a pregnant woman, an infant male child, a dragon, a sea beast, and a land beast. Just as we have seen with the use of apocalyptic images and language, the depictions of the woman, the dragon, and the two beasts are other worldly. All of these characters defy any resemblance to corresponding beings in real life. However, all of them do point to living realities whether to a particular person, an entire empire, an imperial cult, or even various members of the Godhead itself. The only character in the entire episode that is not cast in apocalyptic imagery is the infant male. Although being snatched up to heaven from earth is a very apocalyptic experience, it remains that the infant male child himself is not described in apocalyptic terms.

The scene begins with the sign of a woman in heaven. The woman is clothed with the sun, has the moon under her feet, and a crown of twelve stars on her head. The images of the sun, moon, and stars echo the fourth day of creation in which God creates the sun to rule by day, and the moon and stars to rule by night. These great lights of the heavens were set to rule both day and night, and to separate light from darkness. In the same way that John's vision of the risen Christ at the beginning of Revelation sets the tone and stage for the rest of Revelation, this cosmic image of the woman sets the tone and stage for this centerpiece section.

The fanciful nature of interpretation associated with this particular section is in large part due to the fact that the identities of these characters as they relate to earthly realities are not revealed. There is something of a mystery associated with each of the characters and exact correlations to earthly figures or entities are not offered. The one character who is not couched in apocalyptic language – the infant male child – is also the character that is nearly universally agreed to represent the person of Jesus.

Although the portrayal of the woman as a cosmic figure is quite impressive and also recalls something of the grandeur of the risen Christ in the opening vision of Jesus, the feature that draws the attention of the dragon is that she is pregnant and close to delivery of a male child. The woman is variously interpreted as referring to Eve as the mother of humankind, the nation of Israel as the nation through whom the Messiah was produced, or Mary the mother of Jesus. One of the features of apocalyptic language is that it is polyvalent – it can refer to several realities at the same time. As such, there is even the possibility that the woman refers simultaneously to Eve, Israel, and Mary and the respective roles they each played as "mothers" of the Christ child.

In terms of the story line of this center section, the identity of the woman does not ultimately matter. What does matter is the fact that the serpent is obsessed with the male child that she will give birth to. It is the child whose life is initially in danger and whom the dragon stands ready to devour at the very moment of its birth. However, when the child is born, he is immediately snatched up to the throne of God.

The snatching up of the child at birth to the throne of heaven is undoubtedly the most concise depiction of the story of Jesus imaginable. The story of Jesus is told without a Bethlehem, without temptation and baptism, without disciples, without miracles and parables, and even without a crucifixion and resurrection. It is unquestionably the most slimmed down version of the story of Jesus ever told – he was born and snatched up to heaven.

In contrast to the very uncomplicated story of Jesus is the very complex depiction of the dragon, the sea beast, and the land beast. The features of the enormous red dragon that are most prominent is that it has seven heads, ten horns, seven crowns on its head, and a tail that has the capacity to wipe the stars right out of the heavens and fling them to the earth. The image of the dragon is that of one who has his way with both kingdoms and creation. Seven heads with seven crowns conjure up images of the egregious quest for power and the voracious appetite to have supreme rule over all other nations and empires. The multiple heads and crowns also signify the many lives that the dragon has. Cutting off one head of the dragon will never be enough to halt its dominion over all the earth. The horns are symbols of power. The fact that there are ten of them reinforces the notion that the thirst for power and authority are limitless.

The tail of the dragon has the power to destroy even the stars that fill the night sky. Although the dragon has power to bring about destruction to the furthest parts of creation, there are limits to how far the destruction can go. Hurling down stars to the earth is no small feat. However, the dragon does not appear to have the kind of power needed to rearrange the sun and the moon nor the two-thirds of the stars which were not swept away by his tail. From its seven heads to its mighty tail, the dragon is horrific and terrible. With its heads it reigns over the earth and with its tail it destroys in part the very creation of God.

The role of the dragon in this epic scene is that of an anti-God. His reign is filled with terror and cruelty. He does not rule so that his compassion and mercy can be seen to the far reaches of the earth, but so that his crushing blows and his cursing activity can ensure his reign forevermore on the earth. His dominance is even served by a tail which brings destruction to the beauty and order which God has majestically placed in the world.

The dragon has one simple agenda in the story. With power, might, and strength at his disposal, he lies in wait for one moment – the moment when the male child exits the womb and enters into the kingdom of the dragon. In that moment, the dragon will without mercy devour the child and savor the taste of its victory in its mouth. The destruction of the child will all but assure the victory of the dragon in its perverse pursuit.

What the dragon does not count on is the fact that as soon as the child is born, he is taken up immediately to the throne of God. In an instant, the anticipated plot of the dragon is snatched away from him. Before he could even snap his jaws over the infant, it is as if he had been defanged and stricken with defeat. It isn't the child who is aborted, but rather the agenda of the dragon. Not only has the child been taken right up to heaven and to the throne of God, the woman flees into the wilderness. A war in heaven breaks out between Michael and his angels and the dragon and his angels. The dragon cannot prevail and is thrown down to the earth along with his angels. It is at this point that the identity of the dragon is revealed. He is none other than the ancient serpent, the devil, Satan.

Once the dragon and his angels are hurled down to the earth, the dragon sets out to destroy the woman who had given birth to the male child. The woman goes to a place that was prepared for her and where she would be taken care of for a time, times, and half a time – the same amount of time associated with previous references to three and a half years, 42 months, and 1260 days. The significance of these numbers is that they all represent half of seven years. Seven is a number of completeness and the three and a half years simply refers to a partial season of time. The numbers are not seeking to provide exact chronological time frames. Rather, they point to the activities of certain events unfolding in partial seasons of time.

While in the place of refuge in the wilderness, the dragon seeks to destroy the woman. However, creation itself comes to the aid of the woman and opens up to receive the torrent of death that was intended for the woman. Enraged by the inability to destroy the woman, the dragon then goes off to wage war against the rest of her offspring who consist of the followers of Jesus.

The dramatic images and activities of the dragon enable the readers to see what lies behind the hostilities, persecutions, and martyrdoms of God's people. The imperial rulers of Rome serve as pawns in a much larger cosmic story of destruction and death. Their actions are connected to a much larger world of unseen forces. In fact, the entire Roman Empire can now be seen in light of the grand forces which actually give it life and are bent on the persecution of the followers of Jesus. The spiritual war that is fought on a cosmic scale finds expression on the stage of history.

In contrast to the angel that descends from heaven in a previous vision, there are two beasts in this vision. Whereas the angel stands with one foot on the sea and one on the land, one of the beasts emerges from the sea and the other arises from the earth. The angel who holds the scroll in his hand and straddles the sea and the earth is depicted as nothing less than a glorious ambassador sent by God to bring a message from God. Like the dragon, the sea beast has seven heads and seven horns. However, unlike the dragon the beast has ten crowns on its horns rather than seven crowns on its heads. The sea beast also has blasphemous names written on each of its heads, one of which seemed to have a fatal wound that had been healed.

The grotesque combination of leopard, bear, and lion all in one being is also in contrast to the wholeness and glory of the angel descended from heaven. The temptation is to try to identify the seven heads with Roman emperors. The head that has been fatally wounded and healed is often identified with the exploits of Nero and his return to power after presumably being dead. Although exact identities of the seven heads are not revealed, it is more than clear that the beast from the sea is an ambassador and emissary of the dragon – very much like the angel is an ambassador and emissary of God. Having received power and authority from the dragon, the sea beast is able to strike shock and awe among those who witness his powerful deeds. Because of the authority given by the dragon to the beast, people worship both the dragon and the beast.

John then sees a second beast which emerges from the earth. Although the land beast has two horns, they are like those of a lamb. Rather than the soft and unthreatening bleating of a lamb, the voice of the land beast is like that of the dragon. The land beast exercises all the authority of that given to the sea beast and uses that authority to force people to worship the sea beast. It deceives the people of the earth by performing great signs and orders the people to set up an image of the sea beast whose head had been wounded but now lives.

The images of the enormous red dragon, the sea beast, and the land beast provide a graphic and compelling way to see what lies just under the surface of the Roman Empire, the Imperial Cult, and the animosity of the Roman government toward the followers of Jesus. However, it is much more than just a vision which underlies the first century Roman world. These characters and their activities are also an ongoing picture of the entire course of Christian history. Regardless of the empires of the day, these same hellish creatures are doing now what they have always done.

This centerpiece section of Revelation also reveals the conflict that emerges between the inauguration of the Kingdom at the first coming of Christ and the consummation of the Kingdom at the second coming of

Christ. The in between space is filled with the story of a male child snatched up to heaven and the mayhem and chaos that ensues with the dragon and the two beasts. Even though Christ is snatched up and the woman has fled for refuge to the wilderness, the war wages on. Even though the victory over Satan and evil is assured, the powers of hell still find their way into our present and current world. Satan may know that his defeat is sure, but until it is finalized and he is put away forever, the impact of the cosmic conflict is still deeply felt in our lived experience in the world.

Stepping back just a bit from the vivid imagery, we can also see that the dragon, the sea beast, and the land beast form their own version of the trinity – a trinity that is a vile mockery of the holy trinity of Father, Son, and Spirit. The dragon functions in the role of an anti-God. The seven heads, ten horns, and seven crowns unquestionably reflect the rule and reign of the dragon. His attempt to usurp the very throne of God leads to his demise but he is unwilling to lay down his kingdom, his crown, and his scepter. The only move left for him to make is one in which he discharges the last vestiges of his power in an overt attempt to deceive the people.

This power move of deception is aided greatly by the second member of the unholy trinity – the beast from the sea. Receiving power and authority from the dragon, the sea beast even dons more crowns than that of the dragon. Amid the seven heads labeled with blasphemous names is one head that was fatally wounded and is now healed. This could be nothing less than a sheer mockery of the death and resurrection of Jesus. The sea beast is given power to wage war against God's people even to the point of death. Those who are not written in the Lamb's book of life worship the sea beast. In a very dark way, the sea beast serves in the role of an anti-Christ.

Emerging from the earth is the land beast whose two horns of a lamb are a mockery of the slain Lamb and whose voice like that of a dragon is mockery of being a spokesperson for God. This beast forces the inhabitants of the earth to worship the sea beast. Among the great signs performed by the land beast is the ability to rain down balls of fire from heaven. Because it performs signs on behalf of the sea beast, the land beast furthers the deception that fuels its activity. This beast also gives breath to the image that had been created to honor the sea beast and forces all people to receive the mark of the beast. The resemblances to the coming of the Spirit with fire and causing people to worship the beast with a fatally wounded head which has been healed recalls images of the coming of the Spirit at Pentecost and the role of the Spirit in focusing the newly formed movement on Jesus. In this sense, the land dragon serves in a role that could be described as anti-Spirit.

The famous mark of the beast – 666 – is the number of mankind. In the context of this epic centerpiece vision, 666 reflects the fact that the beast does not attain to the number of God – 777. No matter how much mockery is involved and no matter how much deception takes place, the unholy trinity of fiery dragon, sea beast, and earth beast never arise to that of the holy trinity of Father, Son, and Spirit. The unholy trinity takes every measure and makes every attempt to present itself as the trinity of God. Although many will be deceived into worshipping the unholy trinity, they are unaware that this trinity is nothing more than a mirage and mockery of the true trinity.

Contemporary Reflection

The very simple and succinct depiction of the birth of the male child and the ascent to the throne of God stands in stark contrast to the graphic, complex, and detailed portraits of the dragon, the sea beast, and the land beast. It is certainly no mistake that the contrast between the infant child and the three creatures is so vastly different. The simplicity of the way the story of Jesus is told in this section points to the reality that the combined forces of evil and cruelty cannot subjugate or thwart the purpose and plan of a sovereign God.

The dragon and the two beasts are no match for even the infant child which is taken up to the throne of God. In the macro vision of the grand sweep of redemption, the forces that are so constantly poised for destruction are ultimately humbled and humiliated by the child. From our earthly perspective and experience, it often seems that all we see are the dragons and beasts of evil in our world. It is easy to lose sight of the truth that regardless of how large the forces of power and evil are that loom over and around us, the simple story of God's Son looms even larger. The trinity of hell is ultimately no match for the one infant child that is born and snatched up to the throne of God.

This center section of Revelation reveals in a most dramatic and vivid way the evil forces which lie just beneath the surface of history. Although there is not a literal dragon, sea beast and land beast, the deception and destruction represented by these images are very present in our world each and every day. What often goes unnoticed is that these creatures of evil intent are set against a story of God that features a glorious pregnant woman and the birth of a male child. Here are some insights that will help guide us as we consider the reality of evil in our world.

The story of Jesus is cosmic.

The entire scene involving the dragon and the two beasts is prompted by the birth of a male child who is immediately snatched to heaven at birth. The sign of the dragon does not appear in heaven until after the sign of the woman. Both the sign of the woman and the sign of the dragon are depicted in very dramatic and cosmic images. Although the male child is not described by the same kind of graphic imagery as are the woman and the dragon, the story that is told about the male child is quite cosmic in its own right.

The male child emerges from the woman and in an instant is swooped up to heaven and the throne of God. This brief and concise picture of Jesus' descent to earth and ascent to heaven is cosmic. Without images that are cast in the usual terms of highly descriptive apocalyptic language, the entire Jesus story is told almost as if it were a blip in the large scheme of things. Apart from the fact that the child is a male, there are no other descriptions whatsoever about him.

The lack of description stands in contrast to the very detailed descriptions of the woman, the dragon, and the beasts. There can be little doubt that this is a very intentional moment in the story. Even though the story of Jesus in this collapsed narrative is brief and void of imagery pertaining to Jesus himself, the action that takes place is nothing but dramatic and cosmic. A child born of a woman adorned with the sun, moon, and stars is certainly no small birth event. Neither is it a small matter to be born almost right into the grasp of an awaiting dragon. Furthermore, it is no small thing to be snatched up to heaven. Although the description of the child himself is somewhat meager, the activity surrounding him is quite cosmic.

The cosmic story of Jesus helps to bring perspective to the vast amount of evil that is manifest in the world. It is often easier to see the impact of evil than it is to see the presence of Jesus. Evil appears in large letters written across our world, while goodness often appears as small children facing larger than life monsters. Although it initially appears that the woman and male child will be no match for the dragon, it is in fact the woman and the child who are taken to their respective places of refuge. They are not taken there to leave the world without representation of God, rather their refuge only demonstrates the power and reign of God and his Kingdom. As vast and large as evil is, it does not get the last word. Our small image of Jesus often obscures us from the reality that he does not have to be a dragon or a beast to be the sovereign ruler of the world.

The story of Jesus is incarnational.

Of all the characters in this section, the only one that is rooted in full humanity is the male child. Although the woman is pregnant and experiences the pain of childbirth, she is clothed in heavenly splendor and there is no concern regarding her origin. She simply appears as a sign in heaven. The dragon also appears as a sign without any explanation as to its origin. The two beasts emerge from the sea and from the land respectively.

It is no accident of history that the story of Jesus is incarnational. The entire story line of God's redemptive activity focuses on the very fact that Jesus comes to us by way of incarnation. As the ancient creeds have declared, Jesus is both fully God and fully human. He does not come to us in the form of an angel nor as an unwieldly conglomerate of heavenly creatures. Neither does he simply appear as a sign in the heavens. Nor does he come to us as one who emerges from the sea or the earth.

The uniqueness of Jesus as set against all of the other creatures in this centerpiece section is that he is the only one portrayed as coming incarnationally. He is the only one who is fully human. There is something of a humility about it especially in the context of creatures who are described with such apocalyptic features as the dragon and the two beasts. At first glance, it might appear that the story of the birth of the male child is more of a footnote or parenthesis in light of the cosmic descriptions of the woman, dragon, and beasts. Yet, as it turns out, it is precisely this very humble and very human figure that incites the activity of the dragon and his cohort.

The humanity of Jesus makes him vulnerable to such things as hunger, pain, grief, and even temptation. He also falls victim to the consummate cruelty of evil on Calvary's cross. It is in his humanity that he prays in the Garden of Gethsemane that the cup of death pass over him much like the angel of death passed over the Hebrews. Yet the blood on the doorpost of salvation is his own. As incarnate Savior he endures the forces of hell and the depths of death. His overcoming of the grave is also in terms of incarnation. His resurrection body bearing the marks of suffering are an eternal testimony that the story of redemption is incarnational and that even in the flesh, the victory against evil is won.

The story of Jesus brings out the worst of evil.

Even before his birth, the beasts of hell and their hosts are poised to destroy and devour Jesus. It was their full intent that he would pass right from the woman into the throes of death. In preparing for his coming, hell presented the very worst that it had to offer. The scheme is not to win a mere skirmish or even a significant battle. It is an all-out attempt to win the war with one fell swoop before it has a chance to even get started.

Once the child is snatched up to heaven, the dragon's fury is aimed at the woman and the rest of her offspring. The fury of the dragon against the people of God has known no end ever since the male child was taken to heaven. The time between the two advents of Jesus has been a time of constant and relentless persecution and tribulation. Although the outcome of the conflict between God and the dragon has been decided, the sheer ugliness of the ongoing conflict is beyond description.

The brutality of the conflict with the two-advent framework has been aptly described un terms of D-Day and V-Day. The landing of the allied forces on the beaches of Normandy on June 6, 1944, mark the decisive moment in the war. The invasion was the beginning of the end of the German terror across the entire continent of Europe. Although the invasion ensured the outcome of the war, V-Day did not arrive until May 8, 1945. It was on that day that Germany unconditionally surrendered to the Allies. Although the outcome of the war was known on D-Day, the intensity and brutality of the war is greatest during the time period after D-Day and the arrival of V-Day.

Even after the defeat of Satan, the ravages of war continue. The intensity of the war has never been greater than it is between the two advents of Jesus. The victory is assured, but so is the persecution of the people of God and the ongoing attempt to thwart God's purposes in the world. The very fact that the outcome is determined has only exacerbated the futile attempt of every hellish being to wreak as much devastation as possible until the day of victory is consummated.

The desperation of a defeated foe just prior to the final moment of being vanquished is often the most brutal part of the campaign. Living between the two advents of Jesus represent the season when the desperate activity of the dragon and the beasts is at its height. We live in that very season right now. The agony of desperation is demonstrated in the destruction that we witness in humanity and creation, even as the victory of God and the presence of the Kingdom forever unfold before us.

Wrap Up

The centerpiece section of Revelation begins with two signs in heaven – the sign of the pregnant woman and the sign of an enormous red dragon. The dragon's attempt to destroy the male child at the moment of birth is foiled when the male child is snatched up to heaven and to the throne of God immediately upon his birth. A war then breaks out in heaven between Michael and his angels and the dragon and his angels. Once the dragon and his angels are defeated they are hurled down to the earth where the dragon turns his full attention toward the destruction of the woman who gave birth to the child.

Efforts of the dragon to destroy the woman are completely foiled as she finds refuge in the wilderness and as the angry torrent of the dragon is swallowed by the earth. With the emergence of a beast from the sea and a beast from the earth, the unholy trinity of dragon, sea beast, and land beast seek to destroy the other children born of the woman.

Although this section reveals the characters and forces of evil in their most intense forms, the male child represents a moment of fragility and vulnerability that is only compensated by his rescue to the throne of God. The great irony of this vision is that the enormity and ferocity of the dragon and the beasts is no match whatsoever for the male child.

This centerpiece of Revelation is a graphically apocalyptic depiction of the pervasive and perverse evil that floods our world. Through John's visions we get a glimpse of the enormity and vastness of evil that lie just beyond the veil of our lived experience. The look behind the curtain reveals the ferocity of the representatives of hell and the impact that they have in our world. Yet, the story offers the great hope that one male child who is born of woman and snatched to heaven is fully sufficient to bring about the eventual defeat of the dragon and the beasts and to usher in the Kingdom of God on the earth.

ReImagine

At the very heart of Revelation is the story of the birth and immediate snatching of the infant male child to heaven. In contrast to this very simple and succinct vision of Christ are the elaborate and graphic depictions of the pregnant woman, the dragon, the sea beast, and the land beast. The contrast of images could not be more striking. Reflect on ways that the simple story of Jesus as told in the complex apocalyptic images of the other characters might speak to the simplicity of the Jesus story amidst the mayhem of evil.

The apocalyptic images of the woman, the dragon, and the two beasts are not real, but they do point to historical realities. This represents a primary way in which apocalyptic language functions. Think about how these images depict the realities of a persecuted people of God in the context of a persecuting Roman Empire. In what ways do the apocalyptic images enable us to see the hidden powers behind the historical stage in the first century and even in our own historical contexts of today?

The dragon, sea beast and land beast form their own version of an unholy trinity. As you consider the nature of their relationships with each other, think about ways that they intentionally mirror the holy trinity of Father, Son, and Spirit. In what ways might this challenge your understanding of how evil works behind the historical scene? What connections do you see between current expressions of evil and original expressions of evil going all the way back to the Garden of Eden?

Sixth Image:
The Conquering Christ

Imagination governs the world.
Napolean Bonaparte

The next vision revealed to John flows right out of the seventh and last bowl of God's wrath poured out over the earth. The seven bowl judgments are the last in a cycle of the seven seals and the seven trumpets. In each cycle of judgments, the intensity and the extent of judgment becomes greater. With the pouring out of the seventh bowl of judgment, Babylon the Great meets its final demise.

In this vision, John sees a great harlot riding a beast. The harlot is identified as Babylon the Great. In John's context, Babylon refers to Rome and the entire imperial cult. The very beast which she rides eventually turns in on her and brings about her fall.

Behind the historical curtain of everything associated with the vast Roman Empire are the dragon, the beast, and the false prophet. These are the beings who carry the freight of the entire Roman machine including its booming economy, powerful political structure, military supremacy, and the majestic imperial cult – all of which give life and expression to Rome and fill it with glorious splendor as the envy of the world.

This section concludes with a vision of the Conquering Christ appearing on a white horse with his army dressed in white linen also on white horses. His opposition is none other than the dragon, the beast, and the false prophet along with their armies. This represents the final battle between Christ and Satan and the entire cast of characters associated with him. Without the use of any traditional means of warfare, Christ defeats the unholy trinity of beings in reverse order – first the false prophet, then the beast, and finally the dragon himself, who is Satan.

Behind the Scenes

One of the seven angels who poured out the seven bowls comes to John to show him the punishment of the great prostitute. She has committed adultery with the kings of the earth and has intoxicated its inhabitants. The angel carries John away in the Spirit into a wilderness. John sees a woman sitting on a scarlet beast that is covered with blasphemous names and has seven heads and ten horns. The woman is dressed in purple and scarlet and is glittering with gold, precious stones and pearls. She holds a golden cup in her hand filled with the filth of her adulteries. On her forehead is written BABYLON THE GREAT THE MOTHER OF PROSTITUTES AND OF THE ABOMINATIONS OF THE EARTH.

The woman is drunk with the blood of God's holy people. Seeing John's astonishment, the angel explains to him the mystery of the woman and the beast upon which she rides, which has seven heads and ten horns. The beast once was, now is not, and is yet to come out of the Abyss. Those whose names are not written in the book of life will be astonished when they see the beast.

The seven heads are the seven hills upon which the woman sits. They are also seven kings – five which have fallen, one that is, and another who is yet to come, but for only a little while. The beast is an eighth king who belongs to the seven and is bound for destruction. The ten horns are ten kings who have not yet received kingdoms. Their one purpose will be to give power and authority to the beast. They will wage war against the Lamb, but the Lamb will triumph over them. The waters where the prostitute sits are peoples, multitudes, nations, and languages.

The beast will hate the prostitute and bring her to ruin. They will eat her flesh and burn her with fire. The woman is the great city that rules over the kings of the earth.

Another angel having great authority descends from heaven and declares that Babylon the Great is fallen and has become a dwelling place for demons and unclean spirits. Another voice from heaven compels the people to come away from the woman and not share in her sins. The kings of the earth who had committed adultery with her and the merchants who had done business with her will mourn when they see her fire burning.

John then hears a great roar in heaven proclaiming, "Hallelujah." All of heaven's creatures join in unified praise. Declaration is made that the wedding of the Lamb has come. The angel instructs John to write, "Blessed are those who are invited to the wedding supper of the Lamb." John falls at the feet of the angel, but the angel tells him that he is only a fellow servant.

As heaven opens, John sees a white horse whose rider is called Faithful and True. His eyes are like blazing fire and on his head are many crowns. He has a name written on him that only he knows. His white robe is dipped in blood and his name is the Word of God. The armies of heaven dressed in fine white linen follow him. Coming out of his mouth is a sharp sword with which he strikes down the nations. He treads the winepress of the fury of God and on his thigh is written KING OF KINGS AND LORD OF LORDS.

An angel standing in the sun cries out for all the birds in midair to gather at the great supper of God so that they may eat the flesh of all people. The beast and the kings of the earth and their armies gather to wage war against the rider on the white horse and his army. The beast, along with the false prophet, are captured. The two of them are thrown alive into the lake of burning sulfur. The rest are killed with the sword coming out of the mouth of the rider of the white horse, and the birds gorge themselves on their flesh.

John then sees an angel coming down from heaven having the key to the Abyss and holding a great chain in his hand. The angel seizes the dragon and throws him into the Abyss where he is locked and sealed for a thousand years. After that he is set free for a short time. Those who were beheaded because of their testimony for Jesus come to life and reign with Jesus for a thousand years.

When the thousand years are over, Satan is released from prison and goes to deceive the nations and to gather them for battle. When the army arrives at the camp of God's people, fire comes down from heaven and devours them. The devil is then thrown into the lake of fire where the beast and false prophet had been thrown and where they will be tormented forever.

John then sees a great white throne and the one who is seated on it. The dead. great and small, are standing before the throne and books are opened along with the book of life. The dead are judged according to what is in the books. The sea gives up the dead that are in it and death and Hades give up the dead that are in them. Death and Hades are then thrown into the lake of fire and anyone whose name is not written in the book of life is thrown into the lake of fire.

Historical Stage

An angel carries John away to the wilderness where he sees the vision of the prostitute on the beast. The wilderness is the place where the woman who gave birth to the male child fled to for protection against the dragon in the previous vision. In two other scenes John was also in the Spirit – on the island of Patmos on the Lord's Day and in the throne room of heaven. The wilderness is one of the most significant geographical places in the story of God's people. Moses was in the wilderness when he encounters God at the burning bush, the Hebrew people enter the wilderness after their deliverance from Egyptian captivity, the wilderness is where John the Baptist makes his home, and the wilderness is where Jesus was tempted by Satan immediately after his baptism.

The wilderness theme is not just a geographical location in the Scripture. It also has deep theological and spiritual significance. It is a place where God forms his people, a place filled with various kinds of temptation, a place of protection and refuge. In some cases, the wilderness represents a place of danger and torment where evil resides. In other instances, the wilderness is a place of safety and security. As with the woman who gave birth to the male child, the wilderness here is a place of protection from which John will see the horrific activity of the prostitute who rides on the beast.

The image of the prostitute that emerges in this vision is vastly different than the image of the pregnant woman in the previous vision. Whereas the pregnant woman is clothed with the sun, moon, and stars, the woman who rides the scarlet beast is dressed for seduction that leads her clients to complete ruin and total destruction. The woman that gives birth to the male child is a sign from heaven, the prostitute is a sign of everything that comes from the pit of hell. The whoring prostitute also stands in stark contrast to the vision of the Bride of Christ image which emerges in the upcoming vision.

The prostitute is an apocalyptic image that points directly to the Roman world – the culture, the imperial cult, the religious cult, the political machine, the economic engine, the military might, quest for wealth, sexual immorality, and persecution of followers of Jesus. The entire entity of Rome and all that it represents is summed up in the image of the prostitute. The unquenchable thirst for everything that Rome stands for can only be depicted in terms of a harlot who satisfies the immediate lust of her clients whom she readily turns to victims and captives being led through the portal of death and into hell itself.

The harlot holds in her hand a golden cup that is filled with all the filth of her adulteries. The golden cup that is reserved for royalty and wine is in the hands of the prostitute a cup filled with death and destruction. The mockery of the cup of communion is unmistakable. Whereas the cup of communion points to the reality that the blood sacrifice of Jesus creates a new humanity and a new community, the cup of the harlot points to the reality that the community of Rome is established on the drink of its lust for power, wealth, and sexual exploitation.

Everything that is dehumanizing and degrading is reflected in the tasteless description of the harlot. All those who succumb to the temptation of Roman ideology and life are depicted as committing fornication and adultery with the her. Even kings and merchants beyond the reach of the Roman Empire who do business with Rome are considered to have been enticed by the harlot and fall victim to her ploys of deception. Drinking the cup of everything Rome does not lead to life, prosperity, and peace. The only communion experienced by those who drink of the cup of Rome is the communion of a common fate of death.

Written on her head is the name BABYLON THE GREAT THE MOTHER OF PROSTITUTES AND OF THE ABOMINATION OF THE EARTH. In the world of apocalyptic imagery all of this fits just fine on her head. The writing on her head recalls a previous scene in which God seals his people on their foreheads. It also recalls the mark of the beast – 666 – on the forehands or foreheads of the followers of the beast. The name on the prostitute's head is a clear and open declaration of who she really is. There is no attempt here to identify her as anything but what she in fact is.

The beast that the prostitute rides has seven heads and ten horns. This is the same beast that had come out of the sea. The angel explains to John the mystery of the seven heads and ten horns. The seven heads are seven hills upon which the woman sits. This is a very clear reference to the city of Rome which in fact sits on seven hills. Although the seven kings refer to seven emperors, they are not specifically identified. Five of the them have already come and gone, one is presently reigning, and there is one yet to come. Belonging to the seven kings is the beast itself, who is identified as the eighth king, who is going to be destroyed.

This vision is not a code for readers to determine the identities of the seven emperors. As an apocalyptic image, it serves the larger purpose of conveying the reality that any great city and any rulers they might have are ultimately destined for destruction. The immediate application of the vision refers to Rome and its leaders, but the larger application has a much more universal scope. Simply put, nations and their rulers may loom large on the stage of history at any given time and seem permanently fixed in time, but they are all passing by and their existence can be measured in mere moments. Even the ten rulers who are yet to come represented by the ten horns, rule for only a short period of one hour – a very apocalyptic way of saying that a large succession of rulers altogether occupy a very limited space and time in view of the much larger span of the reign of the Lamb.

In a very unexpected turn of events, the beast turns on the prostitute. The very beast which had supported the prostitute and had assured her success, now becomes her biggest threat and most dangerous enemy. The beast will eat the flesh of the prostitute and burn her body. This dramatic fate of the prostitute at the hands of the beast points to the reality that there comes a time in which evil turns on itself and even consumes itself. All of this happens because it is none other than God himself who orchestrates even evil for his own purposes.

John sees another angel coming down from heaven who declares that Babylon the Great is fallen. The angel has great authority, and the mere splendor of his presence illuminates the earth. Rome is stripped of her former glory, wealth, and power and becomes a wasteland for demons and a haunt for unclean spirits, birds, and animals. The kings, merchants, and seamen who have all drunk her wine mourn and lament her passing. In contrast to the mourning of kings and merchants, there is rejoicing among the heavens, the people of God, and the apostles and prophets. A mighty angel then throws a boulder the size of a large millstone into the sea and declares that the great city of Babylon has been thrown down, never to be found again.

This highly imaginative depiction of the fall of Rome is cast in terms of the fall of Babylon. The Babylonians captured Jerusalem in 586 BC and levelled the entire city. The Temple lay in shambles and the citizens were taken into captivity where they remained for seventy years. Babylon itself fell in 539 BC when the Persians under Cyrus the Great brought Babylon down to its knees. Just like the unimaginable fall of Babylon, the city of Rome would also meet its unimaginable demise.

In the world of apocalyptic language, the application of the prostitute image extends far beyond Rome. The image applies to any empire that rides the back of the beast and draws its life from the powers of hell. The splendor and glory of all such nation is short lived – in the words of Revelation only for "one short hour!"

With the fall of Babylon, a threefold Hallelujah resounds throughout the heavens. First, a great roar in heaven shouts praises for the salvation that God has brought to his people and for the judgment that leads to the condemnation of the great harlot. The twenty-four elders and the four living creatures respond by falling down to worship and proclaiming their own Hallelujahs in response to the chorus of Hallelujahs of the multitude in heaven. A voice from the throne declares for all servants to praise God. John hears again a great multitude like the roar of rushing waters and like loud peals of thunder, shouting Hallelujah – for the Lord God Almighty reigns and the wedding of the Lamb has come.

After the demise of the great harlot, John sees heaven open and standing before him is a white horse, whose rider is Faithful and True. The white stallion upon which the warrior sits is in stark contrast to the fiery beast upon which the harlot rides. In contrast to the drunkenness and adulteries of the harlot, the reputation of the warrior is that of faithfulness and truth. Rather than bringing deception and death, the warrior comes to fight for justice and to wage war. His eyes of blazing fire are in stark contrast to the swollen, bloodshot eyes of the prostitute. The many crowns on the head of the warrior far outnumber the ten crowns on the horns of the beast which the harlot rides.

The name written on the harlot is known by all who see her. One of the names of the rider on the horse is known only to himself. The concealing of the name suggests power and authority. It also reflects the reality that there is no one who has control over him. Strikingly, the rider on the horse is not dressed in traditional warfare armor. Rather, he dons a white robe that is dipped in blood. It appears that blood has been shed before the battle even begins. Although there is a name that is concealed, there is also a name that is revealed. The warrior bears the name Word of God. A sharp sword with which he strikes down the nations proceeds from his mouth. On his robe and thigh are written the name KING OF KINGS AND LORD OF LORDS.

The vision of Christ as a conquering warrior has some very surprising twists and turns. One of the most significant revelations about this image is that it frames a very imminent battle scene for a battle that does not take place – at least in the way we would have expected. The ultimate enemies of the dragon, the sea beast, and the land beast have been identified. We have seen the deception with which they prey upon their victims and the destruction and death that follow them like a tsunami wave. In every imaginable way they stand fiercely opposed to God and his people.

The appearance of the white horse and its rider offers a response from heaven itself against the very forces which lurk behind the story of humanity and provoke the vilest of all evils to break out on the stage of human history. However, there is no sounding of a battle cry or the blowing of trumpets to signal the day of battle. The warrior is accompanied by his followers also riding on white horses and dressed in fine linen, but there is no charge into enemy territory.

It is something of an anomaly that the robe of the warrior is dipped in blood. We can only wonder whose blood is on the robe, how did it get there, and when did this bloody event take place. Once we get our minds wrapped around this cosmic image of the warrior Christ, we can begin to see this image from a new perspective. When John sees this image, it is not so that he can witness the battle between the forces of hell and the warrior from heaven from its beginning. In fact, when he sees the image, the battle has already been won. The blood on the warrior's robe is none other than the blood of the warrior himself. It is the blood of sacrifice in which none other than the warrior himself is the sacrifice.

In the war against the dragon and the two beasts, it is not necessary for the Christ warrior to use any weapon of military might to gain his victory. His victory does not come about because he draws a sword with which he decapitates his arch enemy or with which he thrusts into the heart of his deadly opponents. The only weapon he uses is the word of God which proceeds out of his mouth like a sharp sword. The word of God in the hands of the one who spilled his own blood is more than sufficient to put down the enemy and then to put them away for a very long time. The battle of the warrior was fought at Calvary. The blood represents that which belongs to the slain Lamb, who is now depicted as the warrior King.

The battle of Calvary has already been fought. All that remains is the banquet feast of the Lamb and the putting away of the enemy and its cohorts. In a strange twist to the banquet feast, an angel standing in the sun summons the birds of the air to come to the great supper of God where they can eat the fleshly decay of kings, generals, and their horses, as well as all people who are arrayed against God. This image represents the reprehensible and degrading end for those who feast off the harlot Rome. The very ones who commit such adulteries and drink from the cup of filth are now the ones whose flesh provide the feast for the carrions of the air.

John sees the beast and its minions gather to wage war against the rider on the horse and his army. Both the beast and the false prophet are captured and thrown alive into a fiery lake of burning sulfur. As with the other apocalyptic images of Revelation, the pit of fire depicted here is intended not to be a literal description of hell, but to be an evocative image of the consequences of being aligned against God. The lethal deceptions of the beast and the false prophet on humanity come to a finality as the conquering Christ brings their story to an ultimate end. The rest of those who bear the mark of the beast and worship his image are killed by the sword proceeding from the mouth of the victorious Christ and the birds gorge themselves on their flesh.

Having dealt definitely with the fate of the beast and the false prophet, John sees an angel descend from heaven who will now deal with the fate of the dragon – the ancient serpent, the devil, Satan. This angel has the key to the Abyss and holds a great chain in his hand. The key and the chain point unmistakably to the upcoming fate of the dragon. In the most dramatic depiction imaginable, the dragon is bound by the chain and thrown into the Abyss, which is then locked and sealed. The dragon is unquestionably dealt the greatest punishment conceivable. He is not just thrown into a pit but is bound in such a way that escape is an impossibility.

However, there is quite an unexpected and nearly inexplicable twist to this part of the story. There is a term limit of one thousand years in the case of the dragon in which he will not be able to deceive the nations. After the thousand years of captivity the dragon is set free for a short time. As if there are not enough challenges in seeking to understand the book of Revelation, this one rises to the top of the list. We can only ask why. Why has so much effort gone into the binding of the dragon with a chain and the locking and sealing him in the Abyss if he is to be released even for a short time? What purpose is possibly served by his release?

The arch enemy of God is subdued, and it is shocking to imagine that he will be released as if it were a divine necessity of some kind.

This complex and puzzling moment in the story is unsettling and disturbing. Any reasonable expectation, especially considering the ultimate fate of the beast and false prophet, is that the dragon has met his final moment and his chapter can come to a close without any further ado. Perhaps the greatest mystery of the entire book is now staring us square in the eye. There is no short supply of short-sighted answers to this enigma.

In seeking to move the discussion forward, we must keep in mind what we have been saying throughout this entire journey in Revelation. Revelation is a book replete with apocalyptic images that are aimed at our imagination, not our reason. To literalize the thousand year reign is as egregious of an interpretive move as to literalize the key to the Abyss or the large chain that the angel holds in his hand as he descends from heaven and seeks to bind up the beast. The thousand years is not a literal or chronological span of time any more than other measurements of time in Revelation such as 1260 days, 42 months, or three and a half years.

The thousand year span of time is an apocalyptic way of describing the fact that God reigns fully and supremely, not that he reigns for a thousand years. Satan's release for a short time suggests the reality that although evil is a powerful force, its reign is limited. Although evil cannot be underestimated in terms of its ability to raise its ugly and dreadful head, neither should it be overestimated as a reigning power. Evil may present itself as an indomitable foe, but it all crumbles before the Conquering Christ whose reign far exceeds that of Satan. After his final attempt to deceive the nations of the world and his ultimate failure to defeat the people of God, Satan is thrown into a lake of burning sulfur where he along with his two beast minions will be tormented forever more.

Now that Satan and his hellish cohort have met their final judgment and have been assigned their final destinies, there is one last judgment that takes place. John sees a great white throne and the One who sits upon it. He sees the entire assembly of those who have died standing before the throne as the books are opened. The book is an exhaustive record of each person's deeds. The book of life is also opened. Each person is judged according to their deeds. After giving up the dead which they possess, Hades and death themselves are thrown into the lake of fire. Those whose names are not written in the book of life are also thrown into the fiery lake.

The image of a burning lake of fire is undoubtedly one of the most horrific of all images in the entire book of Revelation. Although the image itself is not intended to be taken literally, the image paints a vivid picture of the reality that Satan will be permanently and irrevocably banished from the presence of God and God's people. He will no longer deceive the nations, and he will no longer bring about destruction and death. He is now consumed by the very weapons that he once wielded in his attempts to thwart the purposes of God and to destroy the people of God. Those whose names are not written in the book of life are those are aligned with the deceiver of nations and the persecutor of God's people. The fate of those aligned with Satan will be the same as that of Satan himself – separation from God. This final separation can only be described in terms of an everlasting death.

Contemporary Reflection

This penultimate vision of Christ in Revelation depicts the final fall of the great prostitute who has filled the world with her immoralities, her idolatries, her abominations, and her adulteries. She rides none other than the beast who is empowered by the dragon. Her overwhelming lure among the nations is clothed in her deception of power, glory, wealth, and lust. She rides through the entire course of human history and the fall of nations lies in her wake.

She thirsts for the blood of God's saints and the filth of her vileness and drunkenness fill her cup – a cup from which the rulers and nations of the world are all to eager to drink. However, her devastation and destruction are as assured as the devastation and destruction she has wrought. At the end of the day, evil is ordained by God to turn on itself.

When it does, the prostitute meets her demise. In her vanity is the vanity of the world, and in her fall is the fall of nations.

Her fall is met with remorse from all who have shared in her drink and have been deceived by her lies. However, it is met with resounding joy from the entire hosts of heaven and the heavenly Hallelujahs reverberate throughout the entire world. The beast upon which she traversed the ages meets its final fate, along with the false prophet and the dragon, at the hands of the victorious and triumphant Christ who conquers the trinity of evil and their entire entourage with the word of his mouth. The only blood that was shed in battle is his own and comes by his own volition.

Translating the demise of the prostitute and the destruction of the dragon, beast, and false prophet, all at the hands of the conquering Christ into how it plays out on the stage of human history is daunting. Here are some insights that will guide us as we seek to see how the war behind the human curtain touches our everyday and ordinary human experience.

Evil is a beastly entity that runs just under the surface of human history.

In the same way that classic arguments for the existence of God have deep philosophical and theological roots, arguments about the existence of evil share the same rootage. Rather than seeking to explain the existence of God or the existence of Satan, the Scripture simply recognizes their reality as other worldly entities both of whom are actively engaged in the drama of human history.

Evil can be thought of as a deadly cancer that attacks the internal organs of the body long before there are outward physical manifestations of its inward destructive prowess. Just as cancer can travel unpredictably and uncontrollably throughout the body, evil can travel just under the surface of the entirety of human history. The use of apocalyptic language and imagery is the most powerful means by which evil can be depicted in terms of such things as an enormous dragon, a sea beast, and a land beast.

Satan is not depicted in Revelation simply as a dark force which seeks to extinguish the light of goodness. Rather, he is depicted in terms of an entity that stands in opposition to God and seeks to thwart God's mission at every turn. Although Satan is not depicted as a person, he is depicted as a living being having qualities of personality and powers that are supernatural. Even with many unresolved philosophical or theological questions about Satan, demons, and evil, there is the unquestionable certainty in the Bible that they are realities who are opposed to God, to God's purposes, and to God's people. The realities of evil which lie just under the stage of human history break out as bursting underground water pipes that quickly flood the story of humanity.

The manifestation of evil emerges in the world order.

The world that God loves is also the world that has been co-opted by the power and presence of Satan and evil. Just as God reveals himself in the context of our lived experience of human history, so does Satan reveal himself on the same stage. Whereas God's revelation is one in which his character of holiness is revealed, and his activity of redemption is played out, Satan's revelation is rooted in deception, disguise, and imitation.

The scope of Satanic activity and evil in the world is not limited to the individual and personal sin that beset us all. In a much larger way, evil has a footprint that reaches into our social structures and institutions. Nothing – not even creation – goes untouched and unmarked by the crushing and pervasive presence of evil in the world. The entire world system and everybody in it are singed and scorched by the fiery and destructive presence of evil. Like a tsunami wreaking havoc over an island, evil crashes against the entire story of humanity. We are helplessly and hopelessly swept away by its powerful currents.

The word of Jesus is the only weapon used against evil.

Great wars require the most advanced weaponry available. The war between Christ and Satan also requires great weaponry. The greatest and only weapon used by Christ in this conflict is nothing other than the word that proceeds from his own mouth. Our very first glimpse of this weapon of war takes place as Jesus is tempted by Satan in the wilderness immediately after his baptism by John the Baptist in the Jordan River.

Satan's temptations are specifically designed to lead Jesus down a path which circumvents the redemptive mission of God. Whereas the redemptive mission entails a cross and cruel death, Satan's temptations entail the materialism of turning stone into bread, the sensationalism of leaping from the Temple, and the politicization of God's Kingdom. Giving into any one of these temptations would have led to the aborted mission of God by displacing the cross with a more *successful* kind of messiahship.

Just as the original seduction of Satan came to Eve in the form of words, so does the assault on Christ come in the same exact way. Recognizing that the words of the enemy are miniature trojan horses filled with the venom of death and hell, Jesus doesn't take one single bite. Instead, he returns fire with words of God lifted right off the pages of holy Scripture. These very words are more than sufficient to turn Satan away and to destroy the nations of the world which are arrayed against Christ.

As followers of Jesus, our weapon against evil is still the word of God. However, it is the Word of God which is none other than Jesus himself. It is not the actual words of Scripture that accomplishes the redemptive mission of God in the world – it is the Word to whom the words point. The authority of Scripture is not in the chanting of phrases or reciting passages in hope that demons will be exorcised and people healed. Chanting feverously the name of Jesus does not squash demons and raise the dead. However, the living Christ has the power to create a new heaven and a new earth and to raise the dead from their mortal resting places.

The Word that we have at our disposal is Jesus himself – not a word on a page, but the Word who is the embodied God in Christ and the resurrected Lord. The defeat of Satan and the ultimate and final destruction of sin, death, and hell are by the Word of God – the Christ who reigns as Lord of Lords and King of Kings. The great reformer and hymnist Martin Luther captures the notion with these words, "one little word shall fell him." The Word that fells him is none other than Jesus.

The victory over evil comes at the expense of the sacrifice of the King.

The rider on the horse along with the armies of heaven dressed in white linen and also on white horses appear before the beast and the kings of the earth along with their armies to wage war. The beast and false prophet are captured and thrown alive into a fiery lake of burning sulfur. The followers of the beast are killed by the sword coming out of the mouth of the rider on the white horse. Satan is seized by an angel who comes down from heaven and is thrown into the Abyss where he is locked and sealed.

Throughout the entire event, there is no mention whatsoever of armies with drawn swords clashing up against each other on a battlefield. There is no mention of the shedding of blood. There are no wounded soldiers strewn across the landscape. The rider on the white horse does not receive a single blow from the hand of the enemy and his army suffers no casualties or losses. Not a single drop of blood on either side falls to the ground. The enemy is not defeated by the sword but by the word which proceeds from the mouth of the Warrior on the white horse.

There is only one thing in the entire vision which indicates that there has been bloodshed. John sees that the robe of the rider on the white horse is dipped in blood. The bloodstains are on the robe before the beast and false prophet are thrown into the fiery lake, before the armies of the kings of the earth are killed, and before Satan himself is thrown into the Abyss. The blood on the robe of the Warrior did not come at the hands of any of those who were captured, defeated, and destroyed.

Rather, the Warrior shows up to battle with his robe already stained with blood. The blood is indeed his own, but it does not come as a result of the final cosmic battle. It comes from a supreme act of self-sacrifice. The Warrior King is also the slain Lamb. The blood is that which he himself gave. The sacrifice was one of self-surrender. It signifies the blood that was shed at Calvary. When the layers are peeled back, it is a sacrifice that is not coerced by whips, nails, thorns, or spears – it is a sacrifice freely offered by none other than the King himself.

The way of the cross is the way of the King. It is also the way of the followers of the King. The way of the cross defies all reason and logic. Those who find their fates nailed to a cross do not do so as a sign of victory, but as clear evidence of their defeat and shame. Those who suffer on a cross are not there for honor but for shame. Yet, in the case of this one King, the cross is transformed unthinkably into an instrument of victory and triumph. Those who follow the way of the cross of the King experience the inexplicable reality that abundant life flows out of the act of surrender and sacrifice. It is precisely in this way – and this way alone – that evil is turned back on itself and is ultimately put down and put away.

Wrap Up

The seventh and final bowl of wrath sets the stage for the ultimate vision of the Conquering Christ. However, the initial attention focuses on Babylon and the prostitute riding on a beast. With the outpouring of the seventh bowl, God remembers the city of Babylon and gives her the cup filled with the wine of the fury of his wrath. An angel then carries John away into the wilderness where he sees a woman dressed as a whore sitting on a scarlet beast with the name BABYLON THE GREAT inscribed on her forehead.

Images of such things as a beast with seven heads and ten horns bearing a woman clothed as a prostitute holding a golden cup filled with abominations and filth, all point to the new Babylon which is none other than Rome herself. Like the Babylon of old which held the children of Israel in captivity, Rome holds the entire world hostage to its hellish agenda. The glory of Rome is in fact underwritten by the beast who carries the city on his back.

Although the apocalyptic images refer to Rome in John's day, they also refer to any Babylons which have emerged on the historical scene even after Rome. The story of any such Babylon is essentially the same. The fall of any Babylon is met with deep lament from those who profit from her economic success, political reach, and military strength. The collapse and fall of such Babylons are met with heaven's Hallelujahs reverberating throughout the universe.

After the collapse and fall of Babylon and the destruction of the prostitute, a rider on the white horse appears bearing such names as

Faithful and True, the Word of God, and KING OF KINGS AND LORD OF LORDS. The beast, the false prophet, and the dragon along with their armies are arrayed against him. Each of them meet their final demise but not as a result of the shedding of blood between their respective armies but by the Word of God that proceeds from the mouth of the Conquering Christ. The only bloodshed is that of the rider whose robe is dipped in blood. The victory over Satan and his cohorts and evil is gained by the self-sacrifice of the Conquering Christ. The battle had in fact taken place on a hill outside of Jerusalem and the victory was assured just three days later.

ReImagine

This section features the graphic image of a prostitute riding a beast who is depicted as making the world drunk with the toxic wine of filth in her cup. Her activities stand in stark contrast to the pregnant woman who gave birth to the infant male and the church as the bride of Christ. Reflect on ways that the image of the prostitute speaks to issues such as political power, military power, and economic power.

Christ is depicted as a Warrior King going up against the arch enemies of the dragon, the sea beast, and the land beast. Although poised as a warrior for battle, the only weapon that he uses is that of his word. The only blood that is shed is that which marks his own robe and is given by his own volition. Reflect on how this image of the victory of Christ plays out in our understanding and experience of God's Kingdom.

The release of Satan from the Abyss after the thousand year reign of Christ poses a significant challenge of interpretation. Satan has already been defeated, and Christ has already won the victory. Although his release is for only a short time, it is difficult to understand the purpose of his release. Reflect on ways that you can approach this dilemma given the nature of apocalyptic language. What does the release of Satan say about the nature of evil?

Seventh Image: The Reigning Christ

Imagination is everything. It is the preview of life's coming attractions.
Albert Einstein

In the final scene of Revelation, Jesus is depicted as the Christ who reigns. The defeat of all of his enemies – including death itself – brings about the consummation of his Kingdom on the earth. As it turns out the consummation is not just the end of things, it is the new beginning of new things. The consummation of all things represents nothing less than the full expression of the original intention of God that all things are reconciled.

The vision of the new beginning with which Revelation ends emerges from the original beginning with which Genesis begins. The new creation of Revelation shares a number of features with the original creation. Eden was a pristine garden that served as the dwelling place of God among his creation and creatures. It was the original tabernacle where God took up residence on the earth. The garden itself was nurtured by four rivers that ran through it. In the middle of the garden was the tree of life. While in the garden, Adam and Eve had full access to God.

In the finale of Revelation, a new Jerusalem descends from heaven to earth. In the midst of the city is a garden which has its own river of life that flows from the throne and its own trees of life on each side of the river. God and the Lamb are so fully present that such things as darkness and death are forever banished. The people of God in the city live in complete harmony with God and with each other. As the story of redemption comes to its close, the story of the renewal of all things is just beginning.

Behind the Scenes

After John sees the great white throne and witnesses the judgment of the dead, he sees a new heaven and a new earth. He then sees the new Jerusalem – the Holy City – descending out of heaven from God prepared as a bride beautifully adorned for her husband. John hears a loud voice from the throne declaring, "Look! God's dwelling place is now among the people, and he will dwell with them. They will be his people, and God himself will be with them and be their God. He will wipe away every tear from their eyes. There will be no more death or mourning or crying or pain, for the old order of things has passed away."

The One sitting on the throne proclaims that he is making all things new and commands John to write these words down, "It is done. I am the Alpha and Omega, the Beginning and the End. To the thirsty I will give water without cost from the spring of the water of life. Those who are victorious will inherit all this, and I will be their God and they will be my children. But the cowardly, the unbelieving, the vile, the murderers, the sexually immoral, those who practice magic arts, the idolaters and all liars – they will be consigned to the fiery lake of burning sulfur. This is the second death."

One of the seven angels who had the seven bowls full of the seven plagues tells John that he will show him the bride, the wife of the Lamb. John is carried away by the Spirit to a great and high mountain where he sees the Holy City coming down from heaven. The city shown with the glory of God, and its brilliance is like a very precious jewel – like a jasper, clear as crystal. The city has a wall with twelve gates and twelve angels at the gates. The names of the twelve tribes of Israel are written on the gates. Three gates are on each side of the city. The city has twelve foundations and written on them are the names of the twelve apostles of the Lamb.

With a measuring rod of gold, the angel measures the city. The shape of the city is that of a cube which measures 12,000 stadia in its width, height, and length. The wall is 144 cubits thick. The wall is made of jasper, and the city is made of pure gold. The foundations of the wall are decorated with every kind of precious stone. Each of the twelve gates are made of a single pearl. The street of the city is made of gold – as pure as transparent glass.

John sees no temple in the city because the Lord God Almighty and the Lamb are its temple. There is no need for sun or moon to shine on it, for the glory of God gives it light, and the Lamb is its lamp. The gates of the city are never shut, for there will never be night there. The glory and honor of the nations will be brought into it and nothing impure will ever enter it. Only those whose names are written in the Lamb's book of life will reside there.

The angel then shows John the river of life that flows down from the middle of the street of the city from the throne of God and from the Lamb. On each side of the river stands the tree of life bearing twelve crops of fruit each month. The leaves of the trees bring healing to the nations. There is no longer any curse. The throne of God and of the Lamb are in the city and his servants will see his face and his name will be on their foreheads. There will be no night nor need for light of a lamp or from the sun for the Lord God will give them light and they shall reign with him forever.

The angel tells John that the words are faithful and true and that these things will soon take place. Upon hearing and seeing these things, John falls down to worship at the feet of the angel. The angel forbids John to worship him and declares that he is a fellow servant with John and with all of the prophets and with all who keep the words of the scroll. All worship is to be directed to God alone.

John is then instructed by the angel to not seal up the words of the prophecy because the time is near. Those who do wrong continue to do wrong, and those who do right continue to do right. When the soon coming Christ comes he will give to each person according to what they have done. He is the Alpha and the Omega, the First and the Last, the Beginning and the End.

Those whose robes are washed are blessed. They have the right to the tree of life and have access to the city through the gates. Outside the gates are the dogs, those who practice magic arts, the sexually immoral, the murderers, the idolaters, and everyone who loves and practices falsehood.

Jesus affirms to John that he has sent the angel to give this testimony for the churches. He is the Root and Offspring of David, and the bright Morning Star. The Spirit and the bride say "Come." Those who are thirsty may come and those who wish to take the free gift of the water, of life may come. If anyone adds to the prophecy of the scroll, God will add to that person the plagues that are described in the scroll. If anyone takes away from the words of the scroll, God will take away from that person any share in the tree of life and in the Holy City.

He who testifies to these things is coming soon!

Historical Stage

In this final section of Revelation, we step right into the world of the reign of Christ. The conquest of his arch enemy and of all of his foes has been accomplished. They have all been banished from the presence of God and are forever abandoned in a place where God's presence is never present. It is this very banishment and abandonment that makes the second death a living hell. Descriptions of fiery pits and burning lakes of sulfur are simply imaginative images that can only seek to approach the devastation and ruin of what it means to live completely apart from God.

The heavenly Warrior who brought about such a cosmic triumph is none other than the sacrificial Lamb of God – a Lamb who defeats the enemy through the sacrifice of himself. The victory that is won by the Lamb is not just a victory that defeats the enemy, it is even more significantly, a victory that secures the full salvation of God's people and of all creation itself. The long arc of redemption that stretches across the entire story of the Bible now comes to its complete and full consummation.

At the very heart of the consummation is the renewal of all things. John sees a new heaven and a new earth. This is not a vision which celebrates an escape *from* the earth, but a renewal *of* the earth. The new heaven and the new earth are one and the same. Heaven is not depicted as a place that is *beyond* us, but a place that is *among* us. There is no notion here that we leave a very cursed earth behind us to go to a very blessed heaven where we can leave all our earthly concerns, trials, and worries behind us. Rather, the new heaven and the new earth emerge as the old order of things pass away.

Interestingly, there will be some things that are not present in the new heaven and the new earth. One of them is that there are no seas. This does not mean that water is not important or that there won't be rivers, lakes, and oceans. It is an apocalyptic way of saying that the chaos associated with the watery underworld will no longer exist. The tumultuous seas will no longer claim the lives of those who attempt to sail them. Terrifying sea monsters will not arise from the dark and stormy waters to assault God's good creation and his creatures. As promised to Noah, the waters will never again flood the earth.

The very same idea is present in John's vision earlier in the book in which he is transported to heaven where he sees one sitting on the throne with a rainbow encircling the throne. Before the throne was what appeared to John as a sea of glass, clear as crystal. The sea of glass stands in stark contrast to the violent and uncontrollable movements of the waters of the seas. As we have pointed out numerous times throughout this book, the images throughout Revelation are just that – mere images. It is not by looking *at* the images that we encounter the story of Revelation, it is by looking *through* the images to the much larger realities to which they point.

The fact that there is no sea also takes us back to the very beginning of the story of creation which begins with God creating the heavens and the earth. In its primordial state the earth was formless and empty, and darkness was over the face of the deep. God's Spirit hovered over the waters. From the very beginning of creation, the waters were associated with chaos, darkness, and death. In the new creation, there are no such waters whose deadly and chaotic movements pose a threat to the new life of a new creation.

The new heaven and earth also have a Holy City of a new Jerusalem that descends out of heaven from God. Yet again, the images do not point us away from the earth but toward the earth in its renewed condition. In contrast to the imperial city of Rome which sought to ascend to the heavens, the new Jerusalem descends from the heavens as a bride beautifully adorned for her husband. The city of Jerusalem depicts the place where God's people dwell. It is somewhat interesting that in this particular image, the city of God's people comes down to earth rather than God's people being called up to the new city. Here again, we see the vast fluidity of apocalyptic language to call us away from our literalistic moorings into far more sublime realities.

In its depiction as the bride of Christ, the new Jerusalem is fraught with images of intimacy and relationship. God's dwelling place is in fact not a place but a people. The powerful imagery points to the reality that in the new heaven and new earth, God himself has a new residence. God resides not apart from his people, but among his people. Previously, John was the only human to be in the immediate presence of God in a place where God was surrounded by four living creatures, twenty-four elders, and myriads of angels. In the new Jerusalem, God's people now have full access to God.

The new access to God is so intimate that God wipes away all tears from our eyes as a parent would for their child. God's presence is so consuming in the new Jerusalem that death itself is nowhere to be found. There is no longer any need for mourning, crying, pain and suffering. The life of God which fills the city banishes any vestiges of such things. All of the dreadful experiences of the old order are completely passed away with the passing of the entire old order itself.

One of the angels who had a bowl of the seven plagues carries John to a high mountain. However, the purpose is not for the pouring out of more plagues – they too have passed away. Just as we have seen how the images of such places as the wilderness and the sea point to certain kinds of realities of human experience, so is it true with mountains. Mountains are associated with the place of God's revelation in a fuller sense. After crossing the Red Sea, God called Moses up to a mountain and revealed to him such things as his commandments and his glory. It was on a mountain where God sent balls of fire to consume the offering of Elijah as he faced off with the prophets of Baal. It was on a mountain where Jesus took Peter, James, and John, and was transfigured as he spoke with Moses and Elijah. Now the angel transports John to a mountain to see the Holy City descending to earth.

The new Jerusalem is filled with the splendor and brilliance of God's glory. The city has high walls and twelve gates on each of its four sides. Angels are posted at each of the gates. The names of the twelve tribes of Israel on the gates along with the names of the twelve apostles of the Lamb on each of the twelve foundations paint a grand picture of God's people from both the old covenant and the new covenant as those who take up residence within the city. The vantage point of seeing the city from a great and large mountain reveals the kind of intimacy that the residents of the city have with God.

The measurement of the city carries a deep significance as seen by the fact that the instrument of measurement is a gold rod. The city is shaped like a cube and measures 12,000 stadia in all directions. This is not an attempt to actually measure the city in terms of distance. As part of an apocalyptic vision, the dimensions seek to provide a theological depiction of the city. If the stadia are translated into literal miles the distance would be roughly 1400 miles. Here is a very clear example of where a literal approach to reading apocalyptic language leads to a total misunderstanding of the significance of the vision.

Measuring the city in terms of 12,000 stadia is filled with theological significance – the actual measurement is totally irrelevant. In fact, thinking about this city in terms of distance is to miss the point altogether. The number 12,000 represents the idea of a city that is complete and secure. The significance of the number 12,000 is related to its factors (12 x 1000). The 12 refers to the fact that there are 12 prophets and 12 apostles, and the 1000 refers to fullness of measure – just as 1000 referred to fullness of time in the previous vision. The walls are measured as 144 cubits in thickness. Again, if this is translated into feet the point is entirely missed. The 144 is derived from the simple factors of 12 x 12. The significance is in what the numbers represent in the context of an apocalyptic vision – not in the actual equivalent in terms of miles or feet. The precious gems of which the walls, foundations, gates, and streets are made are likewise not intended to refer to literal stones, pearls, or gold. Rather, they are used in a much more powerful way to reveal the value of the city in terms of it being the city of God.

When the description of the city of Jerusalem which comes down from heaven to earth is read in terms of apocalyptic imagery, what emerges is not a city that can be physically laid out and described in terms of distances and precious jewels, but a city whose brilliance, splendor, and glory are far beyond measure because it is the place where an immeasurable God resides with his redeemed people. As such, the city is beyond dimension and defies description. The significance of the images is that God dwells with his people, and the city displays a perfect union and harmony of the relationships between God, his people, and all of creation. The grandeur of such a vision is far beyond measure. The measurements only serve to open our imagination as far and as wide as possible to a reality that cannot be reduced to measurements or descriptions.

The most glaring thing that John does not see in the new city is a Temple. There is no place set aside for worship or for the performance of religious observance and practice. It is revealed to John that there is no need for a Temple, because Almighty God and the Lamb *are* the Temple. Every space in the city is filled with the unmediated presence of God and of the Lamb. The presence is so direct that there is not no need for a Temple, there is no need for the sun, moon, or heavenly stars. The glory of the Lord outshines even the sun, and its presence fills the city at all times – there is no setting of the glory of God in the evening and no rising of the glory in the morning hour. There is no longer any need for God to inhabit the holy of holies that is set apart from the people and only accessible by the high priest. There is no need for an altar for the sacrificial Lamb has ended the need for any further sacrifice. There is no need for priestly duties for all who are in the city have been made into a kingdom of priests. There is no fear of sin and corruption for those in the city form a holy nation. Those who do not share in the kind of life which reflects the harmony of God with his people are left outside the gate of the city for they are not written in the Lamb's book of life.

In the final vision of Revelation, the angel shows John a river flowing from the throne of God and the Lamb. The river is none other than the water of life and it flows right down the middle of the street of the city. The tree of life stands on each side of the river. The images of flowing rivers and trees of life are clear throwbacks to where it all began – the Garden of Eden. The four rivers that nourished the original Garden are now represented as one river of life. The one tree of life that stood in the middle of the Garden is now represented by two trees of life that stand on each side of the river.

One of the fascinating features of this vision is that it sets the elements of a garden right in the heart of a city. The images of city and garden are merged together to express the final renewal of all things. These two complementary elements of the vision depict the new city of Jerusalem as a city that is nurtured by a new garden. The image of the city captures the grand reality that all of God's people reside together with their God and with each other in completely restored humanity. The image of the garden is a very powerful expression of the reality that the consummation of the story is a fulfillment of what the original story was intended to be.

The pristine Garden of Eden from the very beginning of creation is now the new reality of God's community. The river that flows from the throne and the trees on each side of the river are life giving. Anyone who drinks from the water of the river and eats from the fruit of the tree experience full and everlasting life. The trees are perpetually fruitful, and the leaves of the tree are for the healing of the nations. No longer is there any curse. Sin and death are forever banished.

The restored Garden is not a mere duplicate of the original Garden. As redemption reaches its climax, the new Garden is in fact better than the original. The long arc of redemption which stretches over the entirety of the story of the Bible is complete. The original Garden which served as a temple and sanctuary for Adam and Eve is now transformed into a new Temple – a Temple not of stone but of flesh and blood.

God and his people and his creation are no longer separated by sin, death, and destruction. All of God's children and all of God's creation experience the full and everlasting impact of being transformed and renewed. In the book that features the revelation of Jesus, it is no wonder and no surprise that the throne of God is also the throne of the Lamb. For the very first time the people of God will see God's face and his name will be on their foreheads and they will reign forever and ever. The greatest of all stories is now told and a new beginning has only begun.

The last matter to attend to involves the scroll itself. John is commanded by the angel to not seal up the scroll because the time of its fulfillment is near. Jesus himself tells John that he is coming soon. Just as the seven churches of Asia Minor in the opening vision were compelled to hear what the Spirit says to the churches, the Spirit and the bride now say, "Come!" Those who are thirsty are invited to drink freely of the water of life. Just as there were warnings for the churches of Asia Minor, now there is a severe warning to any who would add or take away from the words of prophecy contained in the scroll. Those who do so will be met with the most dire of consequences. The final words of the Christ of whom the scroll reveals are, "Yes, I am coming soon," to which John can only reply, "Amen. Come, Lord Jesus."

Contemporary Reflection

Although the visions throughout Revelation leading up to the vision of the reign of Christ are fraught with terrifying and dramatic images of judgment with rays of hope breaking through at various breaks in the scene, the final vision of Revelation brings us into the wide open and unmediated presence of God and of the Lamb. The rays that once broke through the clouds of judgment are now swallowed up by the full force of the sun. The victory of Christ in the previous vision has put away forever the enemies of God in whatever forms they may appear.

Throughout the course of Christian history, followers of Jesus have turned to these final images to find comfort, peace, and hope. There is often a longing in the hearts of God's people for the day in which we experience the realities of the final visions by our escape from the present world which holds us hostage until our final release. Given the reality of the presence of sin, the extent of suffering, and the unending nature of trials, these common sentiments among Christians are somewhat understandable. However, the final glorious vision of Revelation is not a hope that is distinct and separate from our present lived experience.

Eschatology is a present and ongoing reality.

The book of Revelation offers a corrective to our short-sighted notion that eschatology refers only to the future events of God. Most of our approaches to eschatology are focused solely on God's future agenda. As such, they feature such things as timelines, charts, and millennial options. As we have pointed out at the very beginning of this journey, and as we have seen throughout the journey itself, Revelation is simply not interested in any of these matters. These are not the things that arise from the text – they are the things that we impose on the text.

Perhaps the most neglected notion of popular approaches to eschatology is that the future has already begun as a present experience. This reality goes all the way back to the announcement of Jesus as he started his ministry that the Kingdom of God has come. He did not spend his ministry talking about the Kingdom as something that would one day come. Jesus' focus was on the presence of the Kingdom *with* and *through* his very presence in the world. Indeed, the Kingdom did not come in full manifestation with Jesus, but it did break through onto the historical stage in an inaugural way with Jesus.

This very idea has been presented several times throughout the book in terms of two-advent eschatology. The coming of Jesus happens in two parts – something the prophets of old could have never foreseen and something which many of the religious leaders of Jesus' day could not embrace. It cannot be overstated how important it is to approach Revelation from the perspective of two-advent eschatology. A misstep at this significant juncture leads to a trainwreck of interpretations of Revelation that litter the landscape and make it virtually impossible to engage Revelation as it is intended.

Once the notion of two-advent eschatology is embraced, it clears the way of the many issues which draw our attention away from the very person of whom Revelation is a revelation. It also clears away our common notions that Revelation is a book about the future. It is in reality a book about the future as it is presently expressed in our lived experience. Although there are undoubtedly features of the future story that await their consummation at the second advent of Christ, there are also features of the future that are experiencing at this very moment.

The Kingdom of God is a tangible reality.

The beautifully depicted images of the city of Jerusalem and the garden in the middle of the city could not be a more perfect and dramatic way to express the reality of God and his people living in unblemished and untarnished community. Although the images themselves are just images, they point the way to realities that far surpass the images themselves. Those who are chained to a literalistic approach to apocalyptic images will have a stunted view of both the heaven and the hell of which Revelation testifies.

The images themselves speak to our imagination. Although the images themselves face limitations of language, the realties to which they bear witness are tangible. The Kingdom of God is not an abstract theological concept – it is as incarnational as Jesus himself. It functions very much like love itself does. Although there is an intangible mysterious component of love, it is in fact something that we feel and which we express in tangible and physical ways.

The Kingdom as the reign of Christ is not just something that we experience in our hearts or in our souls. Like the strong currents of the ocean, the movement of the Kingdom carries us deep into the world of tangible expression. The currents of the Kingdom are not mere thoughts and theological concepts about the Kingdom, they rush across the stage of history with physical force and reorder the very landscape in which we live.

We are called to participate in God's renewal of all things.

The redemptive act of God accomplished through the death and resurrection of Christ is an act that could only be accomplished through the work of the triune God. There is absolutely nothing humanity has done or could do that could effectively bring about salvation. Although the supreme act of salvation unfolded in the first century world just outside the ancient city of Jerusalem, it was an act that was conceived and executed within and by the Godhead. Although the climax of the redemptive drama of redemption took place in Palestine and was witnessed by Jews and Roman soldiers alike, redemption did not come at the hands of human effort. Jesus gave himself as a sacrificial Lamb and God raised him as a triumphant King.

Although God's redemptive plan for the world does not depend on us, it most certainly involves us. In his death, Jesus bore the sin of the entire world, and in his resurrection he defeated sin, death, and hell for all who follow him. Although the act of redemption belongs solely to God and the Lamb, the followers of the Lamb are invited to share in the renewing effect of redemption in the world. Redemption is much larger than saving people from the consequence of their sin so that they can avoid a hellish eternity separated from God. Our short sightedness at this point – just as our short sightedness concerning eschatology – leads to a vision of redemption that focuses only on eternal destinies.

The final images of Revelation depict a redemption that is so much larger than personal destinies. It encompasses the renewal of all things. Although the renewing process is an act of God through the reigning Christ, we are by God's grace and desire invited to participate in the act of renewal. In other words, we can join God in the act of renewal as participants with God. Salvation is not confined just to a prayer of repentance and a confession of Jesus' lordship. Salvation encompasses so much more – the restoring of broken relationships and the renewal of creation itself.

The renewing process calls us from observation to participation. We don't have to stand on the sidelines or sit in the bleachers. We are invited to get into the game and share in God's renewing work all around us. We could abdicate our responsibility and let God do all the renewing. He is more than capable of doing that, but as a loving Father his desire is to have his children join him in the adventure of renewal. If we choose not to participate, we lose the joy of participating in God's activity of renewal in the world. By accepting the invitation to be partners of renewal, we walk in the fullness of our calling as followers of the Lamb. Rather than seeking to escape the world in which we live, we choose to live in the world in such a way that God's renewing work unfolds through our very frail humanity.

The fulfillment of redemption signals a whole new beginning.

Revelation is obviously and understandably considered to be the final chapter of God's redemptive work in Christ. A story that goes all the way back to the creation itself has now come to fulfillment. The basic story line is quite simple – God created a world that was good, the sin of Adam and Eve introduced death and destruction into God's good world, God so loved the world that he sent his Son to bring about redemption, the redemption will be culminated with the second coming of Christ.

It is natural to think about Revelation as THE END. It is the end of Christ's work of redemption, but it is not the end of the story. In ways that we could have never scripted, Revelation brings us back to the beginning – not the old beginning but a new beginning. In this sense the story has just begun again. In the new beginning, there is no sin, death, and ruin. The throne of God and of the Lamb are at the very center of a world that is recreated and renewed. All enemies are defeated and there is a perfect and harmonious relationship between God and his people.

We are often encouraged to live with the end in view or to even stand in the end as much as possible and live back from the end. These are very imaginative and helpful ways for us to live our present experience from a deeper and fuller perspective. The book of Revelation, however, calls us to an orientation that is like no other. Not only does it invite us to see the story that is being played out in dimensions beyond our human experience, it also invites us to participate in the story of renewal with a new beginning just ahead of us. In the new beginning we shall reign with Christ forever. This is not the kind of reign that is established by military might or political power or economic success. It is not the kind of reign that mirrors the Imperial cult of Rome. Rather, it is the kind of reign that is established by the sacrificial Lamb.

As followers of the Lamb, we can already begin to lean into and live out the reign of the Lamb. However, we must do so with the realization that this reign is built upon the strength of such things as sacrifice, weakness, and vulnerability. The Lamb's reign is shaped by a cross – not by a sword. It is a reign which liberates the oppressed and brings mercy and compassion to those who have been downtrodden. It is a reign that brings encouragement and hope to the marginalized and neglected. It is a reign that offers forgiveness and healing to the adversary. It is the reign of which there is no end.

Wrap Up

The images associated with the reign of Christ are among the most cherished and embraced images in the entire Bible. They bring comfort in times of loss, hope in times of despair, and encouragement in times of grief. Even if everything else in Revelation feels like a dense fog with vague images, the final images come into full and clear view as we descend through the thick clouds, and the early rays of morning light begin to break through the darkness.

The final vision gives us a glimpse into the life that followers of the Lamb experience once the act of redemption culminates. We may not be able to explain what awaits, but we can imagine it. Featured in this reality are a new heaven and a new earth, a Holy City, the throne of God and of the Lamb, a protected community of God's people, and a new Eden. The presence of God is so fully pervasive that there is no need for a Temple or even the sun. In John's initial experience in Revelation, he is transported through a door into heaven. In the final vision, earth is transformed into heaven. All of creation itself joins in the song of praise to the Creator and the Sustainer of all things.

Now that the story of redemption is complete, anyone who dares tamper with the story by adding anything to it or subtracting anything from it will face the most dire of all consequences. The story is of God's making and by his grace do we find ourselves in it as his people who are beloved forever. Although God invites us to partner with him in the dramatic unfolding of redemption, we only do so as followers of the Lamb. The story is not ours to control. We are not endowed with powers of sovereignty, and neither are we charged to make things in our own image. However, we can flow with the perpetual winds and ride the ceaseless waves of redemption.

What an amazing story that brings us all the way to the very consummation of it all only to show us a whole new beginning. As we wait and pray for the coming of our Lord Jesus Christ, we do so knowing that the infinite journey which lies ahead defies even our finite imagination. That which lies ahead is not so much a static world of bliss as it is a dynamic world teeming with new life, evolving relationships, unending wonder, and endless joy.

ReImagine

The opening proclamation of Jesus was that the Kingdom had come (Mark 1:15). Everything that Jesus said and did was directly connected to the Kingdom. Although the Kingdom was inaugurated with the first coming of Jesus, it will be consummated with the second coming.. In what ways does an understanding of this two-advent eschatology impact your present experience of following Jesus in our present historical context?

Consider the connections between the story of creation in Genesis 1 – 2 and the story of new creation in Revelation 21 – 22. These stories serve as the bookends of the entire story of redemption in the Bible. In what ways do you see these two stories related? In what ways do you see the in between stories of the Bible as related the opening and closing stories?

We are much more than just objects of God's redemptive work in the world – we are participants. The invitation to partner with God in what he is doing in the world is a calling for every follower of Jesus. Reflect on some of the practical ways that being a partner with God is manifest through your life and through your community of faith.

Conclusion

Anyone who lives within their means suffers from a lack of imagination.
Oscar Wilde

Revelation is the most thoroughly apocalyptic book in the Bible. The innumerable train wrecks of interpretation that happen to those who dare to read it are mostly related to the lack of understanding concerning the nature of apocalyptic language. This one thing alone has spawned a whole host of interpretations that completely miss the message of the book. Every literary genre has its own unique way of conveying its message. Unfamiliarity with apocalyptic genre is like trying to fit the words of a soft love ballad into a heavy metal score. When we don't understand apocalyptic language we end up forcing the words of Revelation into a genre that is not suitable for apocalyptic language. The end result is fanciful interpretations of Revelation that often make for great book sales, intriguing movies, and compelling sermons, but are worlds removed from the intention of the book itself.

The premise of this book has been simple. Revelation delves deep into the well of apocalyptic images and knocks at the door of our imagination to invite us into its wonderful world of imagery. The world of apocalyptic imagery works both ways – it invites us to enter it while at the same time the images enter us. Although this may sound like nothing other than childhood fantasy to those who insist that reason rules and logic cannot be laid aside, it is in fact the portal that allows us into the depths of both mystery and meaning.

To enter the world of imagination may mean that we lay aside our usual allies of reason and logic, but it in no way means that we lay aside the realities that we encounter in the world of apocalypticism. We are not leaving truth and meaning when we enter the world of apocalyptic images. Rather, we are engaging truth and meaning in even deeper and fuller ways than we could have if we had shut the door to our imagination. Just ask Lucy as she enters into the world of Narnia through the old professor's wardrobe!

We have sought to engage Revelation with the leading edge of imagination. In so doing, we can see that complex timelines and millennial option approaches evaporate before our very eyes. The very popular approaches that gave us handles in dealing with Revelation have in fact led to smoke screens which obscure the very story that Revelation conveys in such imaginative and dramatic ways. It is precisely these kinds of handles that arise out of the innate desire to manage the text and exercise some measure of control over its meaning. However, the images of Revelation simply cannot be managed and controlled. Like Aslan, they cannot be tamed.

By opening our imagination to the text of Revelation, we have allowed ourselves to be more vulnerable as readers of the text. Imagination more easily opens the door to a whole host of human emotions and experiences. When we stop expending our energy in seeking to manage the text, we are postured to have every human emotion and sense imaginable activated. Revelation affords us the opportunity of experiencing everything from paralyzing fear to unfettered freedom, from overwhelming judgment to abounding hope, from tragic defeat to glorious victory.

Rather than mapping out the future, Revelation is far more interested in taking us to the behind-the-scenes drama of spiritual activity so that we may have a fuller and deeper vision of what is transpiring on the stage of human history. Without the behind the scene images, we would be more perplexed and disoriented than we already are as we seek to grapple with the big issues of the purpose of life and the meaning of history.

To dismiss Revelation as irrelevant for such things as spiritual formation and transforming worship would be like taking a diamond out of a ring. We may still have a ring, but we lose the luster and mystery that only comes with a diamond or other precious gem. Revelation is the diamond that captures our imagination and whisks us away to a world of apocalyptic images so that we may in fact engage our present world with faith, patience, love, and hope.

Revelation invites us to recapture the wonder of sacred imagination. It is in the imagination that we can entertain thoughts, feelings, and hopes in ways that are not available to us in any other way. The drama of Revelation is not intended to give us fodder for restrictive analysis and micro level exegesis, but for liberating vision and macro level grasp of the story which is being told. Whereas the usual methods of reading biblical texts tend to shrink the text to bite size pieces, the use of imagination broadens our encounter with the text well beyond our own small vision of the world.

Although the images in Revelation are not the images that we actually see on the historical stage, they are the images *through* which we see human history played out from the perspective of God's redeeming activity in the world – an activity that has none other than Jesus Christ as its centerpiece.

In the very opening words of Revelation, it is made clear that the revelation that is being revealed is Jesus. Our particular approach in this book has sought to identify the various ways in which Jesus is revealed and to read the text in light of these images. The various images of Jesus function in the same way as the various names of God. Just as no one name alone captures the totality of God's being, no one image of Jesus alone captures him completely.

Revelation is a Jesus-centric book that invites us to a world of images. This world is accessed through our imagination and is made possible by the fact that we are made in the image of God. It is precisely being made in the image of God that grants us the capacity to enter into the world of Revelation and by so doing encounter the very Jesus who is the LORD OF LORDS AND KING OF KINGS.

Select Bibliography

Aune, David E. *Revelation*. Word Biblical Commentary. Thomas Nelson, 1998.

Barr, David L. *Tales of the End: A Narrative Commentary on the Book of Revelation*. Polebridge Press: 2011.

Beale, G. K. *Revelation: A Shorter Commentary*. Eerdmans, 2015.

Boring, M. Eugene. *Revelation*. Interpretation: A Bible Commentary for Preaching and Teaching. Westminster John Knox Press, 1989.

Duvall, J. Scott. *A Theology of Revelation: God's Grand Plan to Defeat Evil, Rescue His People, and Transform His Creation*. Biblical Theology of the New Testament Series. Zondervan Academics, 2025.

Fee, Gordon D. *Revelation*. New Covenant Commentary Series. Cascade Books, 2010.

Keener, Craig. *Revelation*. NIV Application Commentary. Zondervan, 2000.

Koester, Craig G. *Revelation: A New Translation with Introduction and Commentary*. Anchor Yale Bible Commentaries. Yale University Press, 2015.

Ladd, George Eldon. *A Commentary on the Revelation of John*. Eerdmans Classic Biblical Commentaries. Eerdmans, 2018.

Morris, Leon. *Revelation*. Tyndale New Testament Commentaries. IVP, 2003.

Mounce, Robert H. *The Book of Revelation.* New International Commentary on the New Testament. Eerdmans, 1998.

Osborne, Grant R. *Revelation.* Baker Exegetical Commentary on the New Testament. Baker Academic, 2002.

Reddish, Mitchell G. *Revelation.* Smyth and Helwys Bible Commentary. Smyth and Helwys, 2001.

Schriener, Thomas R. *Revelation.* Baker Exegetical Commentary on the New Testament. Baker Academic, 2023.

Schussler Fiorenza, Elizabeth. *Revelation: Vision of a Just World.* Fortress, Press, 1992.

Wall, Robert W. *Revelation.* New International Biblical Commentary. IVP, 1995.

Witherington III, Ben. *Revelation.* New Cambridge Bible Commentary Series. Cambridge University Press, 2003.

Other books by Brian Williams

Moneyball Church: Beyond Institutional Reign

Acts: Stories and Backstories

Parables: Common Kingdom Sense

For conference and seminar engagements contact Brian at brian@unscriptedchurch.com

www.ingramcontent.com/pod-product-compliance
Lightning Source LLC
Chambersburg PA
CBHW060833050426
42453CB00008B/683